"I have read several books on angels, and this is my favorite, the best I have read on the subject. And unlike the shallow New Age books on angels, Judith acknowledges that not all angels are good and that some are actually evil in their relationship to humans. She finishes the book on the positive truth about the authority of believers over unholy angels or demons. *Angels Are for Real* is a great, practical, enlightening book."

Randy Clark, founder and overseer,
The Apostolic Network of Global Awakening

"Most of us are blind to the spiritual realities around us. We know little of the unseen realm. We are so fixated on the natural that we don't know what God has given us in the spiritual realm. That's why I am so grateful for Judith MacNutt and the solid, biblical teaching in this book. She reminds us that God is at work all around us, and that He has commissioned His angels to minister to His people. I pray your eyes will be opened as you embrace these important truths."

J. Lee Grady, contributing editor, *Charisma*;
author, *The Holy Spirit Is Not for Sale*

"*Angels Are for Real* is a book that will intrigue you. It is a book that will give you understanding and definition into how the heavenly angels move, minister and bring the message of the Kingdom of God. Judith shares her own stories and stories from others about experiencing the angelic realm. In *Angels Are for Real* you will learn the possibilities of experiencing this realm in your own life."

Pastors Bill and Beni Johnson,
Bethel Church, Redding, California;
authors, *When Heaven Invades Earth* and
The Happy Intercessor

"Thank God for such an insightful and inspired book! The only people who do not enjoy the company of angels are those who do not believe in them."

[Fr.] Richard Rohr, OFM; Center for Action and
Contemplation, Albuquerque, New Mexico

"Judith MacNutt reveals the unseen spiritual atmosphere surrounding us, between heaven and earth, populated with ranks of angels. This is no New Age fad. The stories here are arresting, solidly biblical, personal and practical. They take us into the supernatural realm, pulsating with love and power for us all."

Don Williams, Ph.D.; director, Vineyard Leadership Institute

ANGELS
are for real

Inspiring, True Stories and Biblical Answers

JUDITH MACNUTT

Chosen
a division of Baker Publishing Group
Minneapolis, Minnesota

© 2012 by Judith MacNutt

Published by Chosen Books
11400 Hampshire Avenue South
Bloomington, Minnesota 55438
www.chosenbooks.com

Chosen Books is a division of
Baker Publishing Group, Grand Rapids, Michigan

Printed in the United States of America

Library of Congress Cataloging-in-Publication Data
MacNutt, Judith.
    Angels are for real : inspiring, true stories and biblical answers / Judith
MacNutt.
        p.   cm.
    Includes bibliographical references (p.   ).
    ISBN 978-0-8007-9515-3 (pbk. : alk. paper) 1. Angels. I. Title
BT966.3.M33 2012
235′.3—dc23   2011036928

The Internet addresses, email addresses and phone numbers in this book are accurate at the time of publication. They are provided as a resource. Baker Publishing Group does not endorse them or vouch for their content or permanence.

Cover design by Lookout Design, Inc.

12   13   14   15   16   17   18   14   13   12   11   10   9   8

To Francis,
my beloved husband,
devoted father of Rachel and David,
encouraging, inspiring and loyal companion
whose strength, faith and constant love
have made this journey with God
the most extraordinary adventure of my life.
I love you. . . .

Contents

Foreword

I count it a high privilege to be married to Judith, and we have often talked about encounters with angels. The topic is so interesting that I encouraged Judith to write this book. There are already some excellent books on the subject, and many people think back to Billy Graham's outstanding book *Angels: God's Secret Agents*. Judith's book combines a scriptural study of angels together with experiences that show why angels are important in our journey of salvation. They are not just symbolic; they are real and touch our lives. Teaching on angels goes back as far as Genesis and comes forward as far as this week's television programs. Furthermore, Judith and I are blessed to be surrounded by Christians who have their own extraordinary stories of encounters with the angelic host. Just yesterday, a member of our Christian Healing Ministries staff told us about an angelic encounter.

Over the years, I have often asked groups of people, "How many of you believe that you have personally encountered an angel?" It has impressed me that usually about half of the group will raise their hands. I think that is a remarkable statistic, not to mention a remarkable reality. You might just ask the same question of your own prayer group or of your friends. Just think, in a typical group of people sitting quietly in church, you will probably find, if you draw them out, that about half can tell you about a very personal encounter that they themselves have had with angels. The stories we hear are fascinating, and you will read some of them in this book.

I hope you can learn something in these pages about why the ministry of angels is such an incredible gift to us. Among other blessings, they *protect us, warn us* and *guide us*. I am deeply inspired by how God has helped us over the years by sending us His angels. In reading the stories from Judith's early life and those stories submitted by friends, I was happily surprised. I am not one to cry easily, but as I read Judith's story about finding her father's ring, I was deeply moved.

It is so encouraging to believe that God has appointed an angel to guard us—a guardian angel to protect us from danger and evil of every kind. Generations of Christians have believed this, but most of us hold this belief on faith because angels are usually unseen. Unseen or not, they actively influence our lives in very real ways. Surveys indicate that about half of theologians believe they are real, while the other half believe that they are merely a symbolic way of talking about God's activities.

Judith has written this book because, in addition to believing in angels, you can also experience their actions as they impact your life. I also encourage you to pray in such a way that you may come to recognize their presence in your life as they lovingly act to protect you (guardian angels) or guide you (messenger angels). Even if you do not see angels blessing and helping you, they actually do assist you in extraordinary ways. If you truly believe that God has assigned angels to teach, to protect and to guide you, it can encourage you tremendously in your prayer life when you pray asking for their protection and guidance.

The many testimonies included in this book show how much God loves us, and how, at times, He may even save our lives through the powerful intervention of angels. Learning more about angels will naturally lead you to lift prayers of praise and gratitude to God. Angels are real!

Francis MacNutt

Acknowledgments

To my husband, Francis—you are the glue that has held me together, along with God's grace, for these 32 years. Without your encouragement and love, my gifts would have remained buried. Thank you for always inviting forth what I couldn't see within myself. You offered great wisdom and theological insight, and edited numerous versions of the manuscript. I couldn't have done this without you.

Many thanks to David MacNutt, our gifted and beloved son, who masterfully edited the angel stories. You are my heart! Your encouragement and love helped me to continue when other distractions tugged at my time and heart. Thank you.

Thanks to my friend Kathi Smith, who spent hours typing, researching and offering creative suggestions during the entire process. You are a gifted woman with a loving heart. I am blessed to call you and Taylor friends.

Deep thanks to Gail Mosely, who transcribed and compiled every angel lecture I gave into a working manuscript. Before your gift, the book was only a dream.

Many thanks to Jane Campbell, whose loving encouragement allowed me to believe that my limited knowledge of the angelic realm would be an encouragement to readers. Also, deep gratitude goes to Trish Konieczny, my editor, who became an affirming presence to focus my thoughts into something intelligible on paper. Many thanks to Tim Peterson, who graciously worked with me with the cover design. To Natasha Sperling, who worked to bring this book into being, thank you.

Thanks to the staff of CHM for your loving support and prayers. A special thank-you to Linda Strickland for overseeing the daily operations at CHM while I was writing. Also, many thanks to Lauren Corley for the numerous ways you helped—especially securing permission rights. A heartfelt thanks to our incredible CHM board of directors, who blessed me with time away from CHM to write, and especially to the board chair, Lee Ann Rummell, who graciously shouldered numerous responsibilities. With deep gratitude, I want to thank our national board of directors for your prayerful support. To our CHM staff, both boards, CHM prayer ministers and intercessors—you are our beloved family in Christ Jesus. We love you.

Thanks to all who contributed angel stories. You have encouraged many people with your experiences. Unfortunately, all of the stories submitted could not be used because of space—however, each story submitted brought inspiration.

Many thanks to Katie and Charlie Towers for their lovely beach home and to Thad and Virginia McNulty for time in their beautiful mountain home. From laughing seagulls and lapping waves to eagles soaring over mountains, I was renewed by the wonder of God's creation.

Years ago a box was sent to me from the late Jamie Buckingham. He was a gifted writer of numerous bestselling Christian books. God told him to send his research to me—he said I was the one to write this book. I was deeply touched, and I thank Jamie for his faith in God and in me.

It is impossible to list the names of all the friends who have prayed for and encouraged me over the years. I love you all.

one

A Gift
from My Father

*M*any years ago, before Francis and I married, I experienced an angelic encounter that radically altered my perception of the invisible spiritual realm. Allow me to share with you the mysterious story that opened me up to the world of angels and demons, and ultimately led me to understand more about God Himself.

I had just returned home from a lovely evening with good friends, and I was preparing for bed. The hour was later than usual for me, and I had a full day's work ahead of me at my counseling practice in Clearwater, Florida. During that time, my work days began with early morning prayers at my church, followed by a quick breakfast and then eight to ten hours of counseling with my clients. I loved the quiet times of inner healing ministry to the brokenhearted, depressed and suffering ones who came to me. I delighted at being a small part of the transformation process of their lives. God's great love for each one of them became evident to me and, above all, to them in this process.

Exhausted and in need of a good night's sleep, I began my bedtime ritual—changing into something cozy, brushing my teeth, locking the doors, removing a cross necklace, earrings, a watch and . . . my ring! I stared at my bare ring finger in shock. My beautiful diamond-and-sapphire ring was missing. My heart sank. It had simply disappeared. I had not felt it slip off my finger. How could I have lost it? Where could it be?

Grabbing a flashlight, I began my frantic search—praying all the while, "God, please help me find my ring." I searched my bedroom, every inch of my condo, the sidewalk, the garage and my small sports car. After retracing my path from the car to the bedroom three times, I realized the ring had not fallen anywhere in or around my home or car. Frantically, I phoned the restaurant where I had eaten dinner, asking the staff to search around the table where I had been seated. I then phoned my friends at whose house I had enjoyed dessert after dinner, asking them to look for it. After what seemed like an eternity, the kind restaurant manager and my friends both phoned back to say that my ring had not been found.

I was overwhelmed with sadness at the loss of this precious ring. Unwilling to accept my loss, I wandered around my home, hoping against all odds to find it. Around midnight, I gave up my search. Overcome with grief, I sank into the wicker rocking chair in my bedroom and began to cry. How could I have lost it? Blaming myself became easy. So many questions were tumbling through my mind. The sense of loss became too much. I had such a deep attachment to that ring, and for a very special reason. My mind returned to the warm, sunny afternoon in Nassau when my father had unexpectedly given me the ring.

My dad and I had flown to the Bahamas to celebrate my thirtieth birthday. My older brother, J. C., who was sailing the islands for a year in his sailboat, came to Nassau, too. My dad had not left his home in Kentucky since my mother's sudden death seven years earlier, and I looked forward to this trip as a time of much-needed healing between us. My mom had been the glue that held our family together. Since her death, we had drifted far apart. We rarely saw each other, and when we had come together in the past for the holidays, we felt strained and uncomfortable. Now we were planning to spend an entire week aboard a 55-foot sailboat.

Anticipating the close quarters we would share over the next few days (physically and emotionally) the afternoon before we set sail, I grabbed my dad and pulled him toward the gangplank and said, "Let's go shopping. It's my thirtieth birthday, and I've decided to buy a ring."

Being the rugged mountain man that he was, setting his feet on dry, solid ground again was very appealing to Dad, even though he detested shopping. We wandered through several jewelry stores on the main street before venturing onto a side street and discovering a small and lovely shop owned by a local designer. The rings in the shop were beautifully displayed in a few well-lit cases and were sorted by price. As I had fun trying on the rings that suited my budget, I noticed my dad had walked over to look at the pricier rings.

I selected a small gold ring with a simple floral design, nothing fancy, but unique and beautiful. I called my dad over to get his opinion. After glancing at it, he surprised me when he said, "I don't like it. There's one in this other case I want you to see." He took me by the arm and led me over to the most elegant ring section in the shop. I had glanced at the rings in that case, but had quickly realized they were too expensive.

Pointing to a particular ring, Dad said, "I believe this ring was made just for you." As I began to protest, the clerk quickly removed the ring from the case and handed it to me. Dad encouraged me, "Try it on."

I slipped it on my finger; it was a perfect fit. Never before had I seen a ring that danced with such light and beauty. The ring was crafted with a wide, striated gold band containing a small diamond, and brilliant blue sapphires nestled themselves around the centerpiece. Though I loved it immediately, I twisted it off my finger, mumbled concerns about the expense and handed it over to the disappointed clerk.

I then looked into my father's beautiful green eyes, saw them brimming with tears and saw the pure love that was on his face. He smiled ever so tenderly, took my hand and said, "This ring is my gift of love to you. Whenever you wear it, wherever you are in life, always remember that your father loves you."

As I accepted his "gift of love," my heart began to soften. At that moment, memories of my teen years full of stormy arguments with Dad and painful recollections were forgiven. The little girl inside of me, the one longing to be loved and accepted by her daddy, faced her father in that moment with an indescribable joy filling her heart. The ring became a symbol to me of Dad's love and of our family's healing. The assurance of his love, sealed forever in my heart, was covering the deep wounds I had carried since my teens. This was the threshold of a new beginning for us and for our family. As I remembered the story and was jolted back into reality, I realized that now that precious ring was gone.

As the memories receded, my deep sense of loss returned. Sitting in the darkness, I realized I had to find the courage to surrender my painful loss to God and allow Him to enable me to move beyond my sadness. I vacillated between surrender and sorrow. Loss affects us in this way. My clinical training reminded me all too much of the process of grief in that moment. Sometimes we prefer to cling to our misery, thereby postponing acceptance, release, comfort and healing. I was so afraid that if I surrendered the ring, I would be giving up my father's love. I realize now that those thoughts were not true or logical, but I was not thinking logically during this crisis. I was clinging desperately to what the ring symbolized—not just clinging to the ring. It had served as a constant reminder of a golden moment in time.

At that point, I reached for my Bible. My mother had always said, "Whenever you feel discouraged, read your Bible." I found the passage with Jesus' story of the woman diligently searching for her lost coin. Next I read about the loving father who waited, looking longingly for his lost prodigal son. Slowly I realized that nothing that is "real," such as love, is ever lost. The prodigal son lost all his possessions, but not the beautiful love between his father and himself. Was it possible to stop clinging to the symbol of my father's love, the ring, yet hold tightly to the forever love that was in my heart?

As I prayerfully turned my dilemma over to God, I finally accepted the necessity of releasing the ring—not the love it symbolized. As I prayed, the ache in my heart slowly diminished, replaced by the comforting presence of God. I prayed, "Thank You, Father, for the loving relationship Dad and I have been blessed with—for all the healing You have brought about to restore us. Thank You, too, for the joy of wearing that beautiful ring that symbolized Daddy's love. I release to You my precious ring, and I pray that whoever finds it will also experience the great joy and love I knew."

Leaving my Bible on my wicker rocker, where I had almost fallen asleep, I crawled into bed. I nestled under my mother's warm, hand-pieced quilt. As I settled into the drowsy stillness that precedes sleep, I offered one more prayer. "Lord, You know I've released the ring. If it's not too much trouble, would You send an angel to return it to me?" Never in my life had I prayed for God to send angels to do anything—much less to return a lost ring. Feeling slightly embarrassed by my frivolous request, I drifted off to sleep.

The following morning, my alarm awakened me after only three precious hours of sleep. Feeling somewhat groggy, I rushed to dress so I would not be late for morning prayers at my church. I could still be on time if I moved quickly. As I backed my car out of the garage, I thought I heard a voice saying, "Go back inside; your ring is there."

I knew the ring was not there, however, so I continued on my way. About a mile from home, I heard the voice again, only this time the tone was louder and definitely more insistent: "Turn around and go home."

Feeling somewhat confused, I found a place to turn around, and I headed home. The voice had disturbed me, especially the demanding tone. *Why should I look at home for my ring? I thought. I searched every inch of the place last night, so I'm wasting time. This will make me late for church.*

Upon my arrival, I unlocked the door and entered my silent home, glancing around as I walked through the rooms. When I reached my bedroom, I felt a flash of sadness as I remembered my loss and the drama from the previous night. *Shake it off,* I told myself, *and get on with your day. Coming home was a mistake; go to church.*

Suddenly, I was immobilized by a strange sensation. Something had radically altered in the atmosphere around me. I had not switched on the light, and heavy shades still blocked the early morning sun. I had never been a morning person, so I took great care to maintain a dark sleeping space. Slowly, like the sun rising at dawn, a light crept across the bedroom floor, growing brighter by the moment. Someone unseen who reflected the brilliance of God was there—a holy presence whose brightness seeped into every corner of the room. I was reminded of the sun's light as it reflects off the morning dew—like thousands of tiny diamonds refracting the light and covering the dew-drenched earth.

Feeling slightly uncomfortable with this "presence," I started to inch my way out of the room. As I backed out to leave, a sparkle of dancing light caught my eye. Looking for the source of the sparkle, I walked over to the corner, where I had sat in my rocker the night before. There, on the flowered seat cushion, my Bible lay right where I had left it. I leaned closer to get a better look, and there on top of my Bible, placed by unseen hands, was my beloved ring. Stunned, I thought, *This is impossible.*

Suddenly I felt weak. Tears filled my eyes, blurring my vision. As a psychotherapist, my next thought was, *I must be hallucinating—seeing things and hearing strange voices.* I actually was afraid to reach for the ring. I felt as though I were in a dream. Instead of picking it up, I touched it ever so gently. It was real. I was astonished. It was not a dream or a vision.

Placing the ring on my finger, I laughed and cried at the same time. Indescribable feelings of wonder, awe and joy flooded my entire being. Torrents of praise and thanksgiving to God rushed out of my grateful heart. Never before had I felt so completely alive, or so confused. Then the flood of unanswered questions began. How did the ring get there? I had just been reading the Bible a few hours before; the ring could not have been there. Then I remembered my last request to God before falling asleep—"Please send an angel to return my ring." Was it possible that God had commanded a mighty angel to find it? Did the angel place it on top of my Bible so I would *know* that I could not have overlooked it in my search? Was the insistent voice I heard in the car the voice of an angel? All unanswered questions.

Totally perplexed by these unusual occurrences, I rushed to my car and drove straight to church. The service was still underway, so I slipped into a pew at the back. Opting to skip breakfast and spend time in prayer, I remained on my knees, thanking God and also seeking answers.

As I thanked God for all He had done to bring about this miracle, an overwhelming sense of His presence enveloped me. My questions fell silent as I waited before Him in that sacred space, and then He spoke. His voice, so deeply resonant within me, was full of tenderness and love: *You know your earthly father loves you. I have commanded My angel to bring you this ring because I long for you to know that your heavenly Father loves you, too. This ring is My gift of love to you, too—it is now twice given, and you are doubly blessed.*

Out of that marvelous, life-altering experience, the greatest longing of my heart was fulfilled—to know and to be known intimately by my Abba, my Daddy. *Abba* is the Aramaic word that Jesus used when referring to God. It is the intimate, familiar term used to indicate the closeness of their relationship.

This divine encounter increased and further shaped my understanding of the unseen spiritual realm in which angels dwell. When we embrace the ministry of the holy angels, we begin to comprehend the loving care of our heavenly Father. He created these majestic, powerful beings to be our companions throughout our earthly journey. In the following chapter, we will discover together what an angel is by studying scriptural references, and I will share inspiring, true-life stories of angelic encounters from people just like you.

two

What Is
an Angel?

S everal years ago, while teaching at a conference on healing in Ogunquit, Maine, I thought the Holy Spirit was
directing me to give a teaching on angels. At that time, I
certainly believed in the existence of angels, but I had never
considered teaching or writing about them. I did not consider
myself an authority on the subject, and still do not, so I tried
to change to another topic, one with which I felt more comfortable, more knowledgeable. The longer I prayed, however,
the more blank my mind became. I finally realized that I had
to return to the original topic of angels.

After I spent several hours searching Scripture, an outline
began to take shape. I gave the lecture on angels, but because
of my limited knowledge, I asked the sound technician not
to record the teaching. I did not want it to be publically

available; I was too concerned about my own inadequacy. The attendees, however, were very receptive and seemed extremely disappointed that the lecture had not been recorded. A few years later, I discovered that the sound technician had, in fact, recorded it and had been distributing it at no cost. That teaching on angels became a source of comfort and encouragement to many people. Since that time, I have continued to study angels, and I now realize that their ministry is extremely vital to individuals, to the Church and to the advancement of the Kingdom of God.

Most of the observations I make throughout this book come from Scripture. A few others come from my own experiences with angels, or from the experiences of others. Yet we all agree that angels are real and play an important role in furthering the Kingdom of God.

God created angelic beings before He formed the earth or created humans. Every major religion in the world accepts their existence. They are seen as agents of the divine—supernatural, powerful, loving, wise and devoted to God's service. In his *Institutes*, John Calvin said, "Angels are the dispensers and administrators of the divine beneficence toward us—they regard our safety, undertake our defense and direct our ways."[1] The great church reformer Martin Luther stated that "angels are spiritual creatures, created by God without a body, for the service of Christendom and the church."[2] Classical writers such as Shakespeare, Dante and Milton either mention angels or give us their deeper insights into the invisible realm. Angels have been celebrated in art for centuries. Well-known artists such as Fra Angelico, Leonardo da Vinci, El Greco and Thomas Cole have portrayed various images of angels ranging from pillars of light to

Experiencing Angels

Many times during worship or ministry, as I have my eyes closed, I will feel large, strong hands on my shoulders, head, feet, chest or back, and I will think someone has come up to pray for me. I feel peace and mercy flowing into me, but as I open my eyes, no one is there.

—Anonymous

brightly robed, humanlike figures with and without wings. Angels have been celebrated in poetry, music and books. Artists have portrayed them as mighty warriors defending and protecting, or as compassionate, tender beings offering comfort and encouragement.

During ministry trips to different parts of the world, I constantly meet ordinary people who have had extraordinary supernatural encounters with God's holy angels. These experiences are not rare, but for most people, they are unexpected. Are angels appearing more frequently, or is our spiritual hunger for meaning opening our eyes to God's unseen servants?

A 2007 Gallup poll found that 75 percent of Americans believe in angels and 50 percent believe they have their own guardian angels.[3] Today, however, many theologians de-emphasize the supernatural realm, which includes angels. On the other hand, people are seeking assurance that a loving God and His angelic hosts are actively involved in their day-to-day lives. They want to believe that angels are not only involved with us, but are capable of intervening to bring us assistance.

With our current economic challenges, our fractured social network and the breakdown of the traditional family (with its 50 percent divorce rate), life poses many difficulties. Anxiety disorders, depression and addictions are increasing at an alarming rate and often result in job loss, divorce, suicides and frequent hospitalizations. At the root of many of these psychological disorders is a deep spiritual sickness, a basic loneliness created by a culture detached from a loving God. A comment I often hear in counseling is, "I feel so alone and powerless." Our deepest need is to love and be loved. This comes about through an intimate relationship with God, the source of all love.

St. John of the Cross, a sixteenth-century mystic and theologian, taught that the more misery people endured, the more God gave them mercy. As our miseries have increased, God in His mercy has provided these mighty angels to bring His unfailing love to us throughout our lives. Angels are not meant to replace an intimate relationship with God; they are messengers who convey God's love in real and tangible ways. Their presence brings comfort and strength. An angel is a stepping-stone to the larger reality, God's Kingdom, and ultimately points us to God Himself.

Why learn about angels? One purpose is to teach our families, especially our children. Another is to encourage people who are struggling, to let them know that they have a spiritual companion with them on their earthly journey, that they are not alone and that their angelic companion reflects God's great love for them.

In his *Christianity Today* article "Rumors of Angels," Timothy Jones commented,

Telling the Angels Hello

In vacation Bible school, the second graders were instructed to write a letter to a friend. One boy wrote:

Dear God,

I like Bible school. We have fun.

Love,
Donny

P.S. Please tell the angels hello for me.

—Anonymous

Even among intellectuals, the notion of heavenly visitors strikes a responsive chord. Mortimer Adler, philosopher and editor of the Great Books series, tells how he gave a lecture under the auspices of the Aspen Institute for Humanistic Studies. His topic? Angels and Angelology. "The announcement," he wrote, "drew an audience larger than any I have ever enjoyed in the last 30 years." The experience so moved him that he wrote a book on the philosophical significance of angels.[4]

We long to know more, but we need to exercise caution when learning about angels. Much of the available information is not based on Scripture or on Church teachings. Many New Age books and courses encourage us to contact spirits from the unseen realm, which can ultimately lead to dangerous connections with evil fallen angels. Paul warns the church in Colossae,

Do not let anyone who delights in false humility and the worship of angels disqualify you. . . . Such a person goes into great detail about what he has seen. . . . He has lost connection with the Head.

Colossians 2:18–19

This emphasis on the "Head," meaning God, challenges us to stay focused on God, not on angels who are His servants.

Twice on the island of Patmos, the apostle John fell at the feet of an angel to worship him. Immediately the angel said, "Do not do it! I am a fellow servant with you and with your brothers who hold to the testimony of Jesus. Worship God!" (Revelation 19:10; see also 22:9).

> In speaking of the angels he [God] says, "He makes his angels winds, his servants flames of fire." . . . Are not all angels ministering spirits sent to serve those who will inherit salvation?

Hebrews 1:7, 14

I believe angels on assignment choose to remain invisible if possible in order to avoid this very human response of adoration and worship. Their desire is to serve as messengers for the living God—not to be worshiped. I love to receive flowers, but when they are delivered, I know that the delivery person is only the messenger—the bearer of the gift. Someone who loves me sent the flowers, just as our Father sends us His holy angels, the messengers of His unfailing love.

The Creation of Angels

In writing to the church at Colossae, Paul addresses the supremacy of Jesus Christ over all creation, both visible and invisible. Paul also confirms that the entire universe, including the angels, was created by God:

> He [Jesus] is the image of the invisible God, the firstborn over all creation. For by him all things were created: things in heaven and on earth, visible and invisible. . . . All things were created by him and for him.
>
> Colossians 1:15–16

The psalms also speak about the creation of angels: "Praise him, all his angels, praise him, all his heavenly hosts. . . . Let them praise the name of the LORD, for he commanded and they were created" (Psalm 148:2, 5). God's spoken word in the Creation account revealed that when He said, "Let there be light, and there was light," He spoke and the entire creation came into being (Genesis 1:3). The exact time of the angels' creation is uncertain, but several scriptural references give us clues. The greatest one is in Job chapter 38, where the Lord answered Job by asking, "Where were you when I laid the earth's foundation? . . . while the morning stars sang together and all the angels shouted for joy?" (verses 4, 7). This suggests that the angels were present when God created the world—and that they shouted for joy.

The other clue is in the account of Adam and Eve, who yielded to the serpent's temptation in the Garden of Eden. This timeline suggests that the fallen Lucifer (Satan), the adversary of Adam and Eve, was present before the creation of mankind. The creation of countless angels seems to coincide with the creation of heaven, before the physical earth was formed.

The Nature of Angels

God created angels as a separate class from humans, and they possess higher levels of wisdom, authority and holiness than humans. Their many superior qualities were inherent from the very beginning. Angels are rational, intelligent beings with unique personalities. They display a full range of emotions. Throughout Scripture, references are made to angels expressing joy, sorrow, anger and compassionate love. Jesus said, "In the same way, I tell you, there is rejoicing in the presence of the angels of God over one sinner who repents" (Luke 15:10).

Angels are extremely joyful. We see this the night Jesus was born in Bethlehem. The shepherds heard countless numbers of angels joyfully singing as the heavens split open to reveal their presence. Angels also have the ability to communicate or impart to us what is in their nature, such as peace, joy and patience.

The angels' emotions are not impaired by sin. Our human emotions, as well as our bodies, carry the wounds of sin. This is one of the reasons we experience so much fear, anxiety, anger and sorrow. Angels' emotions function perfectly, the way God intended. Angels are also humble, obedient, patient and pure. They possess a fierce loyalty to God and long to serve Him by obediently ushering in His Kingdom. Angels were given a free will by God, allowing them the freedom to choose and to determine their direction in life. The holy angels remain totally submitted to the will of God, unlike the unholy fallen angels (whom we will talk more about in chapter 8).

The Job Descriptions of Angels

Angels are divine intermediaries between heaven and earth. They are at home in the several layers of heaven identified in Scripture. They dwell in the heavenlies and carry out their assignments on earth and in heaven—according to their classification (which I detail in a later chapter). For now, let's look at a brief synopsis of their duties.

In Scripture, we read about the angels' duties and sometimes their nature, but most passages concerning angels simply describe what they do. Observing their behavior, we see God's marvelous provision for us as He sends these divine friends and servants to accompany us on our earthly journey. Angels wait for their orders to serve God throughout the universe. They are created specifically to serve Him alone. They act in accordance with God's direction, not ours. Angels protect and serve humans as God directs and commands. Whether or not you have ever been aware of an angel's presence or assistance, these mighty agents of God have probably helped you many times.

Angels serve God in a multitude of ways, depending on their classification. The angels of the throne room worship and praise God constantly while guarding His presence, His holiness and His sovereignty. They are intimate, trusted companions who carry out God's directions. This rank is composed of *seraphim*, *cherubim* and *thrones*. This grouping has direct contact with God, faithfully remaining in His presence.

The second group or tier of angels is comprised of *dominions*, *powers* and *authorities*. They are involved in the physical universe (such as earthquakes, tsunamis, hurricanes and other catastrophic events).

The third order consists of *principalities*, *archangels* and *angels*. They are primarily involved in human affairs, and they interact with humans and function as guardians of individuals and groups. These angels are entrusted with tremendous strength, authority, wisdom and love in order to carry out their duties.

Let's consider the angels' primary responsibilities.

1. To return with Jesus

"The Lord Jesus [will be] revealed from heaven in blazing fire with his powerful angels" (2 Thessalonians 1:7).

2. To guard the Church

"The mystery of the seven stars that you saw in my right hand and of the seven golden lampstands is this: The seven stars are the angels of the seven churches, and the seven lampstands are the seven churches" (Revelation 1:20).

3. To execute judgment

"Because Herod did not give praise to God, an angel of the Lord struck him down" (Acts 12:23).

4. To give the Law

Acts 7:53 refers to people who "have received the law that was put into effect through angels" (see also Deuteronomy 33:2; Galatians 3:19; Hebrews 2:2).

5. To exalt, worship and glorify God

Regardless of their classification, the entire realm of angels exists to worship God. In Paul's letter to the Hebrews, he wrote, "Let all God's angels worship him" (Hebrews 1:6). It seems that as they praise God, their lives are eternally renewed.

> Then I looked and heard the voice of many angels, number-
> ing thousands upon thousands, and ten thousand times ten
> thousand. They encircled the throne. . . . In a loud voice they
> sang: Worthy is the Lamb, [Jesus] who was slain, to receive
> power and wealth and wisdom and strength and honor and
> glory and praise!
>
> Revelation 5:11–12

Multitudes of angelic choirs proclaim the greatness of Jesus. They are lost in praise and adoration of their beloved God. What lesson is hidden in the wisdom of angelic worship? Have you ever experienced such burning love and ecstasy? Over the years, many saintly Christians have written in detail about their great joy when lost in worship and how they experience overwhelming bliss. In this next story, a believer who is lost in praise hears the angels worshiping.

Hearing Angelic Worship

Once, after a powerful ministry time during a conference, I was resting in the Lord's presence, stretched out on the floor during a break. I didn't realize I had spent the entire two-hour break on the floor, and friends came by to check on me. I could hear the worship group beginning to warm up, except it seemed they had added new instruments that hadn't been played during the afternoon session. I was lying on the floor against the stage and could not see the stage directly.

Overcome by God's presence, I was physically weak, unable to sit up, so I stayed on the floor and rested while listening to the worship group.

The music and voices I heard were exquisite. I was concerned about being in the way during practice and the upcoming worship time. I asked my friends if this worship group was different from the earlier one. They assured me there was no one on the stage or warming up in the room, and that maybe I was hearing music from the lobby. I insisted that I was hearing a worship group, and I made them prop me up and help me stand so I could see. No one was on the stage.

—Robin Morrison

Angels love being where people are praising God, and I believe the attraction to join us becomes irresistible—or is it we who join them? It is within their nature to continuously praise God. Experience has shown that angels are literally drawn to places where God is loved and worshiped.

6. To act as God's messengers

Both the original Hebrew and Greek words for *angel* mean "messenger." This is one of the angels' primary ministries. They act as intermediaries, divine couriers who bring inspired words from God to His children. They also carry our prayers to our Father. These messenger angels bridge the gap between heaven and earth.

Another angel, who had a golden censer, came and stood at the altar. He was given much incense to offer, with the prayers of all the saints, on the golden altar before the throne. The smoke of the incense, together with the prayers of the saints, went up before God from the angel's hand.

Revelation 8:3–4

Messenger angels bring words of hope, encouragement, strength and comfort. They also announce births, such as John the Baptist's birth and our Lord Jesus' birth. Angels carry messages warning us of impending danger, or they reassure us that all is well. When Paul sailed to Rome to stand trial, the ship passed through a dangerous storm called a "northeaster," and it seemed that all aboard would perish. However, Paul stood before the men and said,

Last night an angel of God whose I am and whom I serve stood beside me and said, "Do not be afraid, Paul. You must stand trial before Caesar; and God has graciously given you the lives of all who sail with you." So keep up your courage, men, for I have faith in God that it will happen just as he told me.

Acts 27:23–25

True to the angel's words, the entire ship arrived safely. The striking part of this account is Paul's calm acceptance of the angel's message. Believers in the early Church accepted angels as trusted companions. Angels were actively involved with the daily efforts of the disciples to spread the good news of the Kingdom.

Also included in angelic messages are interpretations of visions, prophetic announcements, execution of God's judgments and assignments for people to perform specific tasks. The following angelic visit happened to Monica, the wife of one of our Christian Healing Ministries (CHM) staff members, just the week I was writing this. The visit brought a hopeful assurance to Monica and her husband that she was in the Lord's hands. Her husband tells the story:

A Reassuring Visit by an Angel

After an emergency visit to the hospital, my wife and I were very concerned about her health. Upon returning home, my wife woke up in the middle of the night and her bedroom was filled with a brilliant light. She saw an angel standing in the middle of her room. She said the angel only stayed for five seconds, but when he vanished, she was filled with peace, knowing that God was with her and would continue to be with her through her health issue.

—Anthony Knighton

7. *To act as guardians, to protect*

"For he will command his angels concerning you to guard you in all your ways" (Psalm 91:11). God has assigned a guardian angel to guard you throughout your life. Your angel carries a pure and eternal love for you, along with a deep devotion to serving God by helping you. This angel stays with you throughout your earthly journey and then accompanies you to heaven.

Our guardian angels are our companions, chosen by God to guard us, but they also help us in our spiritual journey. Because they behold the face of God, they bring the Kingdom of God closer to us. In the following story, Bob's guardian angel assumed a physical form to warn him of impending danger, thus saving his life.

An Angel Warns a Soldier in Vietnam

My angelic encounter took place in 1967, when I was a Marine in Vietnam. Like everyone else there, I was sometimes put in dangerous situations. One incident, however, stands out boldly in my memory because it involved a definite angelic intervention.

I had driven my lieutenant to Con Thien, a war zone on the DMZ separating North and South Vietnam. (Con Thien literally means "Hill of Angels," a name given it by local missionaries.) While the lieutenant was conducting his business, I waited outside in the jeep. After a while, I saw a lone Marine signaling me to come over. He told me that they were getting "incoming" (mortars, artillery, etc.) that morning around where I was parked. Of course, I moved my jeep. Two or three minutes later came the "Incoming!" cry. I dove into a trench and waited out the attack. When it was over, I saw that the area where the jeep had been parked was completely demolished. When I tried to find my new best friend to thank him for the warning, he was nowhere to be found.

At the time, I did not believe in angels; I just considered myself lucky. Now, as I find myself closer to Jesus, I realize my Marine friend was probably my angel who saved my life.

—Bob Counihan

8. To deliver from evil

The reason the Son of God appeared was to "destroy the devil's work" (1 John 3:8). Mighty angels empowered by God are constantly battling Satan and the other fallen angels. This centuries-old battle, carried out in the unseen realm, will end when the holy angels cast Satan and the demons into "the eternal fire prepared for the devil and his angels" (Matthew 25:41). Until then, every believer is engaged in this spiritual warfare, so we need the protection of God's mighty angels. The following moving account reveals the protection of a young child by the great archangel Michael.

Michael Brings Healing and Protection to a Child

A couple of years ago, my husband and I developed a close relationship with a precious eight-year-old girl. Her family sat next to us in church every Sunday, and she would draw pictures for us during the sermon.

One day at school, she became very belligerent. She was hitting, yelling and spitting at the other children. This behavior was totally uncharacteristic of her. Because of this, the school asked her parents to take her home. Seeking help, her parents had her evaluated by a child psychologist, who diagnosed her as schizophrenic and admitted her to a children's psychiatric hospital.

As a member of my church's healing prayer team, I met weekly with the group to pray for those in need. One morning as we were praying, I had a vision about this little girl. I saw in my mind's eye a figure who I "knew" was the archangel Michael. He was standing in the door of the girl's hospital room, guarding her. He was large in stature and was holding a double-edged sword slanted across the open door to her room, barring any entrance. His eyes were fierce. He was dressed like a Roman soldier, with a short tunic gathered at the waist by a leather belt. The "skirt" of his outfit was made of tooled leather strips hanging down to his knees. He wore sandals that were laced and wrapped around his strong legs. The neck of the tunic was rounded, and the sleeves were part of the shoulder seam. I knew he was protecting this child from some sort of evil. I shared my vision with my prayer group as we continued praying.

The next day, a friend called to say that the girl had been released from the hospital. She was perfectly fine and was back at school being the sweet girl everyone loved. Later when I saw her at church, she leaned over and said, "I have a new friend. His name is Michael, and he takes care of me."

I thank God for this beautiful child's healing and deliverance and for Michael the archangel, who delivered her and guards her still.

—*Prim Brown*

In addition to this child's guardian angel, God had commanded the great archangel Michael to defend her. Michael is the mighty warrior angel that you will meet again in the section ahead on the classification of angels. Michael leads the battle against evil and will destroy Satan at the end of the age.

9. To bring healing

When the archangel Gabriel visited Mary to tell her she would have a son conceived by the Holy Spirit, he also told her to name the baby *Jesus*, which means "God saves" or "God heals" (see Luke 1:31). Whenever we say the name of Jesus, we are reaffirming our belief that His primary mission is to heal us. During His public ministry, Jesus healed countless numbers of people suffering from various diseases of mind, body and spirit; He never turned anyone away. Jesus passed on this gift of healing to His disciples and ultimately to every believer. Healing is a part of our rich inheritance, our gift from a loving God to His suffering children everywhere.

Mighty angels of healing work on assignment from God to bring His healing graces. Because their source is God, they are not limited in power. During the many years my husband, Francis, and I have been in the healing ministry, we have witnessed these compassionate angels of healing ministering in powerful yet tender and loving ways.

Allow me to share a reassuring vision concerning angels and their role in healing. Early one summer during a conference, my husband and I were teaching and leading a prayer for healing, and five people out of the four hundred present reported the following vision to us:

The entire back part of the church faded into the background, replaced by a long, descending golden stairway. Jesus, followed by hundreds of radiant angels, appeared on the stairs and slowly walked toward each person waiting for ministry. With loving tenderness, Jesus placed His hands on the sick and suffering, lingering for a few minutes with each one. He then moved to the next person. Several of the angels following Jesus would remain with the person Jesus had left until everyone seeking prayer had been touched by both Jesus and His angels.

The fact that five different people submitted this same vision in writing confirmed its credibility—plus numerous remarkable healings took place that night. This same vision was reported at four other conferences that summer and has been reported many times since then. Healing advances the Kingdom of God.

10. *To gather the elect and carry us through death*

For the Lord himself will come down from heaven, with a loud command, with the voice of the archangel [Michael] and with the trumpet call of God, and the dead in Christ will rise first.

1 Thessalonians 4:16

When I lived in Jerusalem, I had the incredible joy of working at the Garden Tomb, near Nablus Road outside the Old City. Though the exact location of Jesus' burial site is unknown, this tomb is a very sacred site. The empty tomb is carved out of solid rock, with a larger weeping chamber and a channel for a rolling stone to seal the entrance. Some days after closing time, when the tourists were gone, I would slip into the empty tomb to pray silently and to meditate on the cross, death and resurrection of Jesus. Most of those quiet times were spent weeping for what Jesus had to endure for us or joyfully praising Him for the empty tomb and His victory over our ancient enemy, death. Several times, angels would make their presence known either through a fragrant holy presence or a glowing light over the slab of rock that was Jesus' resting place. Angels seem to linger in the Garden Tomb to help those who come there seeking the risen Lord.

In his book *Angels*, Billy Graham wrote,

> Just as an angel was in Christ's resurrection, so will angels keep us in death. Only one thin veil separates our natural world from the spiritual world. Christ both vanquished death and overcame the dark threats of the evil fallen angels. So now God surrounds death with the assurance of angelic help to bring pulsing life out of the darkness of that experience for believers. We inherit the Kingdom of God![5]

People have told me countless stories about angels appearing to collect a loved one at the moment of death. Angels escort us into the Kingdom of heaven, where we are met by loved ones who have gone before us—and finally by the Lord Jesus Himself. C. S. Lewis believed that heaven is in another dimension—so we pass from this earthly realm to the heavenly realm with our angelic escort. The following story is shared by one of our dearest friends, Emmy, who reveals the beautiful passing of her beloved mother.

A Mother's Heavenly Escorts at Death

My mother had been diagnosed with emphysema, and her doctors believed she only had a short time to live. My husband, Frank, was active as an Episcopal bishop of Florida, and our lives were quite busy. Even so, we wanted to be with her, so we moved her into a lovely condominium near our home.

My mother was an incredible believer, having had her life transformed by the power of the Holy Spirit, and she was excited to live close to Christian Healing

Ministries. I would often go into her home and hear Francis MacNutt's voice on tape and wonder if he was visiting her, which, thankfully, he did many times. Because of her deep faith, the MacNutts and many of the community of the faithful, my mother experienced a very holy death. She was not afraid to die. In fact, she looked forward to joining my daddy and others who had gone before her.

My friend Sue would often play her harp, and we would all gather around my mother's bed and sing praise music. Once Mother bolted straight up in the bed and said, "Am I dead yet? This dying is not bad at all."

One day, Bishop Frank had a Diocesan convention and wanted to bring Mother Holy Communion before the meeting. When he walked into her bedroom, she said, "Emmy, did you see that angel fly in over Frank's head when he opened the door?" I hadn't seen it, but she clearly had.

Frank gave her Communion and prayed with her. A few hours later, Mother called me into her room and said, "Emmy, do you see those angels in the corner of my room? There's a path of beautiful flowers on either side, and the street is lined with many, many angels." The picture was so vivid to her. As I sat quietly by her bed, she said, "Emmy, the angels—do you see them now? They want me to come and go with them. I believe I am ready to go; please come hold my hand and help me join them. Wait! Honey, call your brother to be with us." As we stood on either side of her bed, she said, "I am ready to join them." She quietly departed with the angels.

I remember singing, "This is holy ground." And holy it was—the room was filled with the heavenly hosts. After that experience, I will never be afraid of death again.

I was prepared for this time through teachings we had received from the MacNutts and Father Frank Dearing, a local beloved Episcopal priest. We learned that healing takes many forms. In my mother's case, as in the case of many I have known, death was a friend. Death for her came gently, beautifully and in the presence of the holy angels. Blessed are those who have had the privilege of learning to expect them. Angels are real, if we only have eyes to see them.

—Emmy Cerveny

My husband, Francis, and I are privileged to know and love the Cerveny family. We vividly remember the circumstances surrounding the death of Emmy's mother, Mrs. Pettway, and her vision of angels preceding her death. She was a woman of deep faith who approached death as she had approached most things in life—without fear. She understood perfectly well that for a Christian, death is a transition to a fuller life—not an end.

three

How Angels
Appear

*M*any angelic encounters are experienced by the heart, rarely through the normal channel of the senses. Being blind and deaf from birth, Helen Keller lived in a world of quiet darkness. Out of that lonely place, she sought and found a deep spiritual connection to the invisible realm. Later in life, she said that the most beautiful things in life cannot be seen or even touched, but must be felt with the heart. After having heard so many stories of angelic visitations, I have come to realize that angels appear in many different forms and are not always visible to the human eye.

The writer of Hebrews describes angels this way: "He makes his angels winds, his servants flames of fire" (Hebrews 1:7). And "Are not all angels ministering spirits sent to serve those who will inherit salvation?" (verse 14). The Greek word *angelos* means "one who is sent, a messenger who does the bidding of God." Thomas Aquinas, the "angelic doctor"

A Lovely Presence

Arriving home from church one evening, I walked into the bedroom and felt as though I had walked into something. I could not see anything, but my husband was able to see a form floating near the ceiling. I put my hands up and could feel a presence. It was a beautiful feeling. I must have walked right into an angel's foot.

—Anonymous

who lived in the thirteenth century, wrote that angels are pure spirits not composed of matter or form. In the spiritual realm, angels' bodies are pure spirit, unseen by us, although they have density and occupy space. Angels can be experienced in three ways: as *invisible*, as *visible* (the traditional angelic form), and appearing as a *human*. Let's look at these three ways in a little more detail.

Invisible Angels

When God sends angels to help someone in need, they often remain invisible, yet the person feels an incredibly holy presence. Billy Graham stated that "angels are created spirit beings who can become visible when necessary."[1] A few years ago, during one of our Schools of Healing Prayer, a humorous thing happened to Bill, one of our students who was a therapist. Bill was attending our school in order to help his clients. About the third day of class, Bill realized that he needed prayer regarding some painful childhood memories.

Several prayer ministers prayed with him for over an hour. As a result, he experienced a deep inner healing that left him feeling wonderfully transformed, but physically drained. As I was away from Christian Healing Ministries that day, a staff member offered to let Bill rest on the large couch in my office. After resting, he was preparing to return to the class, but he noticed several family photographs on my desk. Out of curiosity, he decided to have a look. As he approached my desk, he ran directly into an invisible, solid wall. He moved slightly to the right, then to the left, but the wall remained. He stepped back to think about what this could possibly be when suddenly several large angels, standing shoulder to shoulder, appeared in all their splendor. They were circled around my desk. Their arms were crossed in a protective posture and their faces were somewhat serious, as if to say, "You cannot come near her desk."

Bill immediately backed away and quickly left my office. When I returned to our center a few days later, he timidly approached me and asked my forgiveness for invading my privacy. Then he told me the story about the angels he saw in my room. I was thrilled to know that angels were guarding my desk, and I assured Bill that he did not need to ask forgiveness. This is an example of angels changing from an invisible form to a visible and very physical form in an instant. Bill had never had an angelic encounter before this, but he was forever changed by this experience.

In this remarkable encounter, we recognize an angel's ability to transform from an invisible being to a visible being at will. The invisible, impenetrable wall was enough to stop Bill, but for some mysterious reason, the angels decided to allow Bill to see them. The angels appeared not as human beings, but as mighty, radiant angelic beings carrying out their assigned duty of protecting my office. Now every time I work at my desk, I entrust myself to their protective, loving care.

Stories like Bill's transcend our understanding but force us to look beyond the physical, visible realm to the unseen, invisible presence of the Kingdom of God surrounding us. Our awareness is elevated to the realm of the Spirit, where the ongoing battle between good and evil is continuously waged—especially by the holy angels. Paul shows that he understands this unseen battle and warns us in Ephesians:

> Put on the full armor of God so that you can take your stand against the devil's schemes. For our struggle is not against flesh and blood, but against the rulers, against the authorities, against the powers of this dark world and against the spiritual forces of evil in the heavenly realms.
>
> Ephesians 6:11–12

This "heavenly realm" is the invisible realm of the Spirit. We access this realm by nurturing a deep, contemplative prayer relationship with God or by simply being given the pure gift of having our eyes opened by God.

Over the centuries, many contemplatives who have delved into the deep mysteries of faith have written about their remarkable encounters with angels and demons and have learned wisdom through their extraordinary experiences. Simply because many in the Church ignore this realm does not indicate that it does not exist. Not only does it exist, but it is an essential truth of the Kingdom of God.

Paul also writes to the church in Ephesus that they "must no longer live as the Gentiles do, in the futility of their thinking. They are darkened in their understanding and separated from

Invisible Comforters

Our four-year-old granddaughter was spending the night at our house and had carefully prepared a spot for us to sleep on the floor. She doesn't sleep away from home often, and she was a little anxious, so we snuggled up close together. We were face to face, but not quite touching. She closed her eyes, and after a while she began to relax, saying, "I'm okay now, Grandma. You don't have to rub my back anymore." With her eyes closed, she didn't know that I was not rubbing her back. Her angels must have been soothing her fears.

—Anonymous

the life of God" (Ephesians 4:17–18). The "futility of their thinking" refers to humanity's natural dependence on logical, rational thinking, which may result in intellectual pride. It also tends to ignore the supernatural manifestations of the Holy Spirit such as healings, deliverance (from demons) and the appearance of angels. Individuals can possess knowledge about Christianity while totally rejecting the supernatural realm, thus being "darkened in their understanding and separated from the life of God."

Notice that Paul did not say "separated from God," but "separated from the life of God." The "life of God" embraces the actions of God incarnate, through Jesus. Simply consider for a moment one day in the life of Jesus. How did He spend His time? In the gospels, references to His remarkable life give us a glimpse of His compassionate love in action. Every day, Jesus taught about the Kingdom of God, but He also demonstrated the power and authority of that Kingdom by healing the sick, casting out demons and raising the dead. Jesus then equipped His followers with this same power, which is for all believers—even you.

Paul's understanding of this invisible realm challenges us to open our eyes, the eyes of our heart (spirit)—which are often cloudy, murky and enveloped in mist, cut off from this glorious reality of angels and ultimately from God Himself. The following story illustrates that the invisible realm is often felt during times of deep communion with God. The story I share after that comes from my own experience at a time when an angel intervened to save my life.

Angelic Visit at Christmas

On Christmas Eve, I was in church at the Communion rail, having just received the elements. I had my eyes closed in deep prayer when I became aware of a person next to me. At first I thought it was my mother, who is shorter than I am, but this person seemed very tall, strong and generally powerful. I continued standing in line with my eyes closed in prayer.

Even though I sensed that the person next to me was still there, when I opened my eyes, no one was there. Everyone had sat back down, and the thought that flashed through my mind was, My angel . . . my guardian angel . . . *he was standing next to me during communion. Overcome with emotion, I cried soft tears of joy and gratitude for this Christmas gift from the Lord.*

—Lorraine Greski

Saved in an Alfa Romeo

Upon my return to the United States after my time in Israel, I settled into a beautiful and warm jewel of a community in Clearwater, Florida. The Christian churches there were vibrant and strong, so I quickly developed loving relationships with several young adults and wise elders who provided the structure and focus I needed to continue my spiritual growth. My home was a small, three-room apartment in a shaded area on Oak Street very near my new friends. I quickly formed a rather loose-knit community with them that blossomed into deep and lasting friendships. We shared meals in each others' homes, prayed together, went to movies and the beach together, and celebrated life's joys and sorrows together. We were an extended family of friends. Life was good.

Shortly after this move, I purchased a small convertible Alfa Romeo sports car. What else would you want to drive where the sun perpetually shines? The convertible top was hardly ever in the closed position. Somehow I released all my concerns when I drove that little car. I felt free with the warm sun on my face and the wind whipping through my long hair.

One lazy Saturday afternoon, I was driving through downtown Clearwater with a good friend, heading to the beach. After a long week of work at my counseling practice, I was definitely ready to listen to the sounds of the beach with its waves, laughing gulls and children squealing in the water.

I was approaching a blind four-way intersection and could see that I had the green light. There was no need to slow down, and I was almost to the intersection when I heard a stern male voice that said, "Stop."

I glanced at my girlfriend and asked, "Did you tell me to stop?"

She looked at me out of the corner of her eye without answering, and again I heard "Stop." But I could not see any reason to stop. There was no one in front of my car, nor behind it.

"Stop!" I heard the voice speak with great urgency. Although I had the legal right to go through the intersection, I abruptly stopped the car just as I was entering the intersection. Approaching from my left on the main street, I saw an enormous Cadillac going at a remarkably fast speed. It almost brushed the front bumper of my little car as it sped through the red light. Had I not obeyed the command to stop, the Cadillac would have plowed directly into my door, crushing me, my friend and my little car. I am certain both of us would have died on the spot.

My girlfriend released a sob, she was so stressed. I could not even move for a few minutes. All I could think was that we had been saved from being smashed like a bug on the street. I then realized that an angel had saved us. I quickly asked my friend if she had heard a male voice urging me to stop. She had not heard the voice. Only I had heard it. We spent the remainder of the day at the beach, thanking God for His invisible guardians who surround us.

What did I learn from this experience? Angels are magnificent beings who are wonderfully persistent. I

*decided that in the future, I would immediately listen
to their warnings.*

Visible Angels—the Traditional Form

Christmas has always been my favorite holiday, ever since I
was a little girl. I love celebrating in simple ways the birth of
our Lord Jesus, and I have spent much time visualizing what
that first Christmas must have been like. So when I moved
to Jerusalem, I could not wait for Christmas Eve to arrive. I
wanted to go to Bethlehem and witness firsthand what the
present-day celebration there was like.

I still remember how my friends and I stood in a long
line at the Arab bus station in Jerusalem, waiting our turn
to catch the bus to Bethlehem. Nothing, not even the frigid
weather, could dampen my enthusiasm. Finally our turn
came, and we climbed aboard an ancient Mercedes bus that
groaned ever so loudly as it pulled onto the highway toward
Bethlehem.

Even though our destination was only a few miles away
and we had left with plenty of time to arrive before dark,
the bus inched along slowly, like a large, ancient turtle with
all the time in the world. I remember thinking we could have
walked to Bethlehem more quickly. Occupying the broken seat
next to me was an older woman who was completely covered
in beautifully embroidered garments. She held a very smelly
goat in her lap, just as I might hold a lap dog. I did not realize what a strong odor goats had. For the remainder of the
trip, I proceeded to hang my head out the cracked window
in order to avoid the strong smell and breathe fresher air.

We finally arrived in Manger Square, which was teeming with people, lights and loud music. The atmosphere was more like a carnival than a celebration of the birth of Jesus. Somehow I had imagined candles, soft Christmas carols and people prayerfully waiting. To escape the commercial atmosphere, we walked a short distance to Shepherd's Field, where we knelt on the damp, soft grass and waited. I kept looking at the sky, expecting at any moment that the heavens would split open to reveal a great company of angels proclaiming the good news of great joy. Looking around the darkened hillside, I could vividly imagine the shepherds of so long ago huddling against the cold rocks of a cave or seated around campfires to stay warm . . . sheep munching on grass with the little tinkling bells tied around their necks softly ringing . . . the distant sounds of other pasture creatures seeking shelter and food . . . the shepherds protecting their flocks, some sleeping while others watch . . . complete darkness except for the crackling fire.

Then, without warning, the heavens split open and the shepherds are enveloped by a blinding light such as they have never seen before. For a moment, they cannot see anything as their eyes adjust to the brilliant and intense light. Then the sound of celestial music reaches their ears, music never before heard by humans . . . indescribable harmonies, voices with incredible range . . . instruments that far surpass our harps and lyres . . . sights and sounds beyond belief.

The shepherds then realize that the glorious light is actually the brilliance of angels, who loom large over the field . . . thousands upon thousands glorifying and praising God with one voice . . . the darkness of the night sky fully illuminated with God's glory . . . seraphim, cherubim, powers, archangels, all shining with the light of God . . . unable to contain their joy. A brilliant angel joyfully proclaims to the shepherds,

> "Do not be afraid. I bring you good news of great joy that will be for all the people. Today in the town of David a Savior has been born to you; he is Christ the Lord. This will be a sign to you: You will find a baby wrapped in swaddling clothes and lying in a manger."
> Suddenly a great company of the heavenly host appeared with the angel, praising God and saying,
> "Glory to God in the highest,
> and on earth peace to men on whom his favor rests."

Luke 2:10–14

Angels from the throne room of the almighty, eternal God delivered this incredible message about the birth of the long-awaited Savior of all humanity. This amazing "press release" was given to simple, uneducated poor shepherds, forever changing our human destiny that glorious night.

Shepherding was one of the lowliest jobs in those days, yet the angels did not release the message to kings or government officials, but to simple "nobodies" to show how much God cares about each and every one of us. "Do not be afraid!" the angel proclaimed to them. Visible angels often tell us not to be fearful. Their appearance often startles those to whom they appear. Daniel's strength left him when he saw an angel, so that he trembled and could hardly breathe (see Daniel 10). Who would not react with some kind of adrenaline surge when an unearthly, radiant being appears? Angels proclaim the message "Do not be afraid!" for good reason.

Late that Christmas Eve, I left Shepherd's Field with a renewed determination to spread the good news about Jesus. I returned to the chaos of Manger Square, ready to reach out and share His great love with those souls who were seeking the baby born in the manger—seeking the great Messiah, God incarnate.

Angelic Form

Thomas Aquinas reasoned that angels could assume whatever form was needed to complete their assignment. Since they are pure spirits and lack form, they can choose to materialize in what can be described as "heavenly bodies." Eyewitness reports vary widely in their descriptions of angels. Some angels appear taller than twelve feet, some smaller. Some appear with wings, others without. Some display various colors in their garments, skin tone and hair.

I have heard angels' wings described as "tissue paper" and "see-through gray" and "almost filmy." Some commonly reported characteristics are that angels appear as bright and shining images like lightning; that they are filled with light, have burning eyes and have voices that sound like thunder or rushing rivers. They have an energy or power emanating from within that causes humans to faint as though dead.

Do you remember the image of Gabriel when he appeared to Daniel? The archangel was dressed in linen, with a belt of the finest gold. He had a body like chrysolite, a face like lightning, with eyes like flaming torches, with legs like the gleam of burnished bronze and a voice like the sound of a multitude (see Daniel 10:4–6). After the resurrection, the angels at Jesus' tomb were described as having clothes that gleamed like lightning (see Luke 24:4).

Angels Ahead

A couple of years ago, I occasionally started seeing a group of angels on the road ahead of me as I was driving. They looked as though they were side by side, holding hands and just standing on the road. The first time I saw them, I sensed that they might signal danger ahead and that I should slow down. When I came to the spot where the angels had stood, an animal was crossing the road.

This vision of angels has been repeated many times. I have seen them for icy patches on the pavement and other road hazards. Once the danger was a group of snowmobilers who darted out in front of me.

—Anonymous

During his exile on the island of Patmos, the apostle John gave us another description of a powerful angel:

> Then I saw another mighty angel coming down from heaven. He was robed in a cloud, with a rainbow above his head; his face was like the sun, and his legs were like fiery pillars. He was holding a little scroll, which lay open in his hand. He planted his right foot on the sea and his left foot on the land, and he gave a loud shout like the roar of a lion. When he shouted, the voices of the seven thunders spoke. And when the seven thunders spoke, I was about to write; but I heard a voice from heaven say, "Seal up what the seven thunders have said and do not write it down."
>
> Revelation 10:1–4

Do you see the similarity in these reports? These Scriptures give us some idea of what the heavenly bodies of angels look like.

Angels in the Early Church

There was a man named Cornelius who lived in Caesarea, captain of the Italian Guard stationed there. He was a thoroughly good man. He had led everyone in his house to live worshipfully before God, was always helping people in need, and had the habit of prayer. One day about three o'clock in the afternoon he had a vision. An angel of God, as real as his next-door neighbor, came in and said, "Cornelius."

Cornelius stared hard, wondering if he was seeing things.

Acts 10:1–4, The Message

The angel then instructed Cornelius to invite the apostle Peter to his home to share the good news of the Gospel with the Gentiles. This was new territory for Peter (as well as for Cornelius), being ordered to extend the Church to include Gentiles. Before the men met, God gave Peter a vision in which He instructed Peter to embrace what he had previously considered unclean. God spoke to Peter three times in the vision, instructing him, "Do not call anything impure that God has made clean" (Acts 10:15). These instructions were so contrary to what Peter believed that it took three visions to convince him.

As the vision ended, three men from the house of Cornelius arrived requesting that Peter accompany them to Caesarea. The Holy Spirit had already spoken to Peter in another vision, telling him to expect these men and go with them. They traveled to Cornelius's home the following day. A small group of Gentiles had gathered to hear Peter present the story of Jesus' life, death and resurrection.

While Peter was still speaking these words, the Holy Spirit came on all who heard the message. The circumcised believers who had come with Peter were astonished that the gift of the Holy Spirit had been poured out even on the Gentiles. For they heard them speaking in tongues and praising God.

Acts 10:44–46

Peter ordered all the new Gentile believers from the household of Cornelius to be baptized in the name of Jesus Christ.

What I love about this passage is that, first of all, Cornelius saw an angel, believed the angel and then carried through and did what the angel ordered. Remember my story about the angel telling me to "Stop"? My familiarity with angels was so lacking that I was wondering where the voice came from, and then I almost defied the voice's message. The early Church seemed to experience angel appearances so often that when angels appeared, the believers did not go into endless theological debates as to whether or not they existed.

Secondly, God's desire was to expand the early Church by embracing the Gentiles. Due to Peter's deeply ingrained beliefs about clean and unclean foods, Peter had to hear directly from God three times in a vision to convince him to go outside the Jewish nation to include Gentiles, who had been defined as unclean. A mighty angel of God set in motion the miracle that was needed to expand the early Church.

In the following story, God allows a mighty angel to manifest himself to a devout man who desired a greater awareness of the spiritual realm.

A Man Sees an Angel after Asking God

Driving home one night from a prayer meeting, I was unnerved because one of the women in our group had either seen or felt the presence of an angel, and

I was starting to feel as though I was missing out on something. My wife and I were newly baptized in the Holy Spirit, and I believed in angels but had never had an angelic encounter.

Later that night, my wife and I knelt down together to pray at the foot of our bed. We went through our usual litany of prayers, which always included a request for angelic protection for our home and family. My wife quickly fell asleep after prayers, while I read.

As I read C. S. Lewis's Screwtape Letters, *I became aware of another person in the room. I was completely awake and alert as a large, handsome male figure entered the room through the wall. He was dressed in a white robe, and he stood from floor to ceiling—nearly eight feet tall. His demeanor exuded peace. He stopped and acknowledged my presence by nodding at me, then he continued walking out of our bedroom through the wall, into the room where our children were sleeping. I shook my wife and said, "Did you see that?"*

She, of course, said, "See what?"

As far as we are aware, there were no problems at the time that made such a visit necessary. God simply pulled back His curtain between our reality and the spiritual realm and let me see one of His holy angels.

—Karl M. Rose

When angels appear in their heavenly form, we are captivated by their holy, radiant presence. Two dear friends of mine, Rose Marie and Sue, share their experiences in the next two stories, where a glowing angel enters with an assignment from God just at the right time for both women.

A Radiant Angel of Comfort

I was involved in a very painful legal battle, and one day I had to meet six lawyers and a court reporter to prepare a deposition. I knew this meeting could be ugly, and I struggled with anxiety and dread. In my quiet time, I prayed to turn my fear over to the Lord, asking Him repeatedly, "Please, just don't let me feel alone."

In the conference room the day of the meeting, I closed my eyes briefly in prayer. Opening them, I immediately saw a large angel glowing with a bright light. The angel was just a glorious being, and I couldn't stop smiling. I knew it meant I was not alone, that God had sent an angel to be with me. He had answered my prayer.

—Rose Marie Edwards

A Vision of Angels Tending a Friend at Death

Some years ago, I had a brief but powerful encounter with angels. It was snowing outside, and I was sitting in my kitchen when, without any warning, I "saw" four angels. As I watched them, I could see that they were beautiful, androgynous looking and tall. They were dressed all in white, and I sensed that they were "tending" to my friend, Archabbot Leopold, at Latrobe Abbey in Pennsylvania. Leopold had been my spiritual director for years, but we now lived in differ-ent parts of the country. The angels were two by two in formation around Leopold's resting body—two at his head and two at his feet, as if they were preparing him for something. Then, only moments later, the vi-sion was gone. I called the abbey, and they said that Leopold had just passed away.

—Sue Saint Sing

Angels Appearing as Human

One time our secretary phoned us in California, where we were giving a conference, and asked us to pray for Jim. He was the husband of a prayer group member and had expe-rienced a life-threatening heart attack. She explained the urgency of his condition, so we immediately prayed on the phone together, asking God to release His healing power to Jim's heart and to send healing angels to be with him. We also invited the conference attendees to intercede for him.

What happened later that night is a powerful testimony of God's love. Jim was drifting in and out of consciousness, gravely ill. In the middle of the night, a radiant presence in his hospital room awakened him. He looked and saw Fran-cis—whom he assumed to be my husband—at the foot of his bed. "Francis" had his arms extended over Jim and was deep in prayer.

Surprised, he called out, "Oh, Francis!" The being he thought was Francis just looked at Jim and held his hands out in prayer. Immediately Jim felt peace, and a gentle warmth filled his body. Jim knew he should rest. He went to sleep, but woke up three times during the night. Each time, "Francis" was at the foot of the bed with his arms extended in prayer, and the radiant presence remained in his room.

When the doctors came in the next morning, Jim was calmly sitting up in bed. He felt wonderful. The doctors ran some tests on his heart and discovered that Jim had a normal, healthy heart—one completely restored by God.

When Jim's wife arrived at the hospital and saw Jim resting peacefully, she asked her husband, "What happened?"

Her husband excitedly replied, "Francis came and prayed for me all night."

She said, "Oh, my goodness. He came all the way from California to pray for you?" She quickly called our office and enthusiastically related the story of the previous night to our secretary. "Please tell Francis that my husband, Jim, has been totally healed. We are overjoyed and thank God for his faithfulness. Please thank Francis for making the long trip."

Our secretary replied, "I didn't know Francis was going to fly back here." This surprised her, so she called us in California just to see if we were still there. When I answered the phone at the hotel, she asked me, "Did Francis fly back to Florida last night?"

I thought it was an odd question, but I responded, "No, he was here all night."

Our secretary said, "Well, he was praying with Jim at the hospital all night, and now Jim has been completely healed."

At first I was surprised, then I realized what God had done. He had sent an angel to minister to this very ill man, and the angel took on the appearance of Francis. I started laughing and said, "That had to be an angel—and it was an angel with good taste."

In this instance, the angel assumed a familiar appearance, someone with whom Jim would be very comfortable, and that was Francis. Jim's wife usually attended prayer meetings alone, but after that healing experience, Jim was by her side every week. This encounter radically transformed Jim's life and his relationship with God. "Do not forget to entertain strangers, for by so doing some people have entertained angels without knowing it" (Hebrews 13:2).

In some cases, in order for angels to perform their duties and move undetected among people, they will assume physical bodies. They may be either male or female, old or young, of varying races and with differing languages or cultural characteristics. Stories are abundant about a being in human form appearing at the exact moment necessary to alter or defuse a dangerous situation, to change the course of a life or to comfort a grief-stricken soul. These angels rarely call attention to their angelic identity; they tend to remain anonymous. Often they disappear abruptly when their task is complete, and yet somehow the footprint of heaven is left forever.

Three men appeared to Abraham while he was sitting at the entrance to his tent near the great trees of Mamre. His wife, Sarah, was traveling with him, along with his servants and herds. When Abraham saw the three men, he immediately invited them to rest and to eat with him. In Abraham's day hospitality was expected, especially toward strangers. Abraham ordered his servants to prepare the finest foods, and before eating, he washed the feet of his guests.

Since women did not eat with men, Sarah was standing near the entrance of the tent, listening to their discussion. When one of the men inquired after her whereabouts, Abraham said she was nearby. One of the men then gave him the

An Angel Polices a Deserted Street

I was in New York with my daughter, and we were trying to find our way back to our hotel on foot. We wandered into a dangerous section of the city, onto a deserted street, but then saw two rough-looking men. We knew we were in trouble when they went out of their way to approach two lost women.

As they came closer, we could sense their intense hostility. We began to panic when, with no warning, a tall policeman appeared on the scene and walked right in front of the two men, blocking the way toward us. The two men took off at a run. As quickly as he had appeared, and without a word to us, the policeman disappeared. I believe an angel helped us that night.

—Anonymous

great news that by that time the following year, Sarah would bear a son.

Since Sarah and Abraham were well advanced in age, and since she had never given birth before, this prophecy seemed absolutely impossible. Sarah's response was to laugh. One of the men immediately asked why she was laughing, and she denied it. And yet, despite her unbelief, God was setting in motion the development of the nation that would become Jesus' family. It started with a visit from three angels who predicted the birth of Isaac, beloved son of the aging Sarah and Abraham. Within the year, Isaac was born. With God all things are possible.

Attempting to conceal their angelic identity, angels who appear as humans quickly disappear directly after their mission is completed. Sometimes they vanish in front of the onlooker's eyes. Often a person will look away for a second, only to find the angel who was disguised as a man or woman has simply left with no visible escape route. Incidents such as these often leave people confused and cautious about sharing their experiences. Over the years, many good people have quietly asked my advice following such an angelic encounter. They want to know if they are going crazy. After quietly relating their story, they seem relieved to discover that someone finds their story believable. I find it helpful to explore with them the results of their encounter. Was it positive and life changing? The majority of storytellers respond positively to their angelic encounters and are deeply grateful to God for the transformation that followed their life-altering event. Most are simply worried that others will judge them harshly or ridicule them for believing in such a remarkable encounter.

Why would an angel deliberately choose to remain anonymous? We must remember that an angel's mission is to fulfill God's instructions while remaining in the background as much as possible. An angel appearing as a human is much less frightening than a luminous, brilliant and mighty angel who has flaming eyes and a voice like thunder. Powerful appearances such as these usually create fear and uncertainty. The entire focus can rest on the angel, not the message or the mission. In Scripture, when angels appear in a traditional way (in their heavenly bodies), people respond by fainting or, at the very least, by falling prostrate on the ground before the angel.

Many warnings exist about the human tendency to go too far and worship the angels. These "otherworldly" beings inspire adoration and worship not only because of their awesome outward appearance, but also because of their intimacy with God. They carry the glory of God in their very presence, and thus usually inspire awe. Paul, however, admonished early Church believers, telling them to avoid worshiping beings created by God. In his letter to the church at Colossae, he expressly forbids the worship of angels (see Colossians 2:18; see also Romans 1:25). He goes further in warning believers to avoid false teachers who teach false doctrines. Angels quickly deflect any worship that is directed toward them. They always remind us to adore and worship God alone.

I am reminded of the response of an angel who had rescued a woman from a dangerous situation. She was expressing her appreciation to the angel for his help, and the angel immediately responded, "Don't thank me; thank God who sent me. I'm only the messenger."

Our dear friend Edna told us the following story. At the time she received her angelic help, she was working for us as a nanny, which she did for a year and a half. Edna traveled with us and came to our home every day because she knew we needed help.

One night Edna, who was 73 years old, was driving from Daytona Beach to Orlando, Florida, on Interstate 4. Although the distance is not far, it was late at night and she was worried about being out alone on the highway. Halfway to Orlando, a tire blew out. She pulled off the road and got out of the car. As she waited she prayed, "Dear Jesus, I need help. Please send someone to help me."

Within a few seconds, an old pickup truck pulled up behind her car. She said she could not believe it was able to move. It had rust everywhere and made a terrible groaning noise. A very nice-looking young man dressed in torn jeans and a rumpled T-shirt got out of the truck, came over and nodded, smiling. He never said a word. He simply got down on his knees, changed the tire, stood up and smiled at her again.

Staring into his eyes, she said, "I know who you are." She did not ask, "Are you an angel?" She simply said, "I know who you are." Edna prided herself on being direct.

The young man smiled even more broadly, got back into his pickup truck and, apparently just for effect, the pickup truck with the young man inside just vanished into thin air.

Edna shouted into empty space, "I knew you were an angel sent by God!"

The angel could have waited until Edna had driven away before disappearing, but he seemed to want to have a little fun with her. From experience, we have discovered that angels have a fantastic sense of humor and exude great joy. Here's another delightful story a woman tells about receiving unexpected angelic help.

An Angel Lifts a Huge Piece of Marble

A friend of mine had carved a beautiful statue of Mary for our church, and we were brainstorming about how the statue should be situated on the grounds. I remembered a piece of marble that had been sitting by the roadside in a neighboring town for about ten years, and I thought it would make an excellent base for the statue. Never having lifted marble before, and without considering the weight of a sizable chunk, I volunteered to drive over and pick up this abandoned piece.

The next day, my friend and I drove the twenty minutes, ready to make quick work of obtaining the slab. It was larger than I remembered, measuring about four feet long by four inches thick. We got on either side of it, braced ourselves and lifted with all of our might. The slab didn't budge. There we were, two women who did very little heavy lifting, trying to lift this stone behemoth. Looking up and down the deserted road, I realized there was no way for the two of us to move it. At a loss for a solution, we sat on the hood of my car.

After a few minutes, a young man on a bicycle rode up and asked if he could be of any help. Half joking, I said, "Only if you could lift this marble into the car."

He smiled, laid his bike down on the grass and walked over to the slab. Without hesitation, he cheerily rolled the marble end over end until it was just beside the open car door. Then, in a display of prodigious strength, he bent down and lifted it into the car. My friend and I heartily thanked him and asked if there was any way we could repay him.

"Just do something nice for someone else," he replied, picking up his bike. Leaving us with that simple request, he waved and rode off.

Later, when we got the marble back to my house, I asked my husband and two sons to help bring it into the church. I told them a boy had lifted it for us earlier, and that it was in the car. When they came home from church after dropping it off, they could not understand how a single person had lifted the marble. The three of them could barely lift it together. I told my husband more about the good Samaritan who had stopped to help us, how he had showed no sign of stress, or even of real exertion, while lifting the slab. He had not even been an especially strong-looking fellow.

I do not know what form angels usually take when they visit us, but on that day I believe an angel came to us as a boy on a bicycle.

—Joanne Weber

Angels appearing in human form have extraordinary strength, such as in the gospel accounts of the angel rolling away the two-ton stone that sealed the tomb of Jesus following His death and burial. Matthew wrote, "An angel of the Lord came down from heaven and, going to the tomb, rolled back the stone and sat on it" (Matthew 28:2). The women who had gone to the tomb early that morning had asked each other, "Who will roll the stone away from the entrance of the tomb?" When they arrived at the tomb, not only was the heavy stone rolled away, but angels were waiting for them with a joyful announcement: "He has risen! He is not here" (Mark 16:3, 6).

The young man in the previous story appeared on his bicycle just as the two women were waiting for God to supply a solution to their dilemma. How interesting that the young man effortlessly rolled the marble slab and lifted it into the car, when Joanne's husband and two sons could barely lift it together. This next story tells how our dear friend Norma experienced help from an angel at a gas station.

Gas Station Help

Some of you might remember a time when gas station attendants pumped gas for their customers. We would simply pull into a gas station and stay in the car while the attendant filled the tank. When attendants became obsolete, there was a time of transition when we had to learn how to pump our own gas.

Silly as it may seem now, I was not comfortable with this change. I didn't know which grade of gas to use, how to turn on the pump or how to pump it. To add to my discomfort, one day I was driving my husband's unfamiliar car. I pulled into the gas station along one of the busiest four-lane streets in the city and braced myself for the ordeal. Standing beside the car, I stared at the gas pump. A panic came over me because I realized I didn't know what to do. Suddenly, at the height of my panic, an old rattletrap car pulled off the busy road and sidled up alongside me. A man was driving, and a young girl sat beside him. After rolling down his window, he called out, "The pump you want is that one."

I turned around to see which pump he was pointing to and thought, How does he know what I need and why did he pull off a busy road to help me? *I turned to thank him, but he was gone—along with the car and the little girl. I stood there trying to sort out what had happened. That is when I realized he was an angel sent by a loving God to help His daughter in need.*

—Norma Dearing

Angels possess the remarkable ability to appear in whatever form is necessary to accomplish God's purposes. In a following chapter, we will discover the numerous classifications or ranks of God's mighty angels. We will begin with the majestic throne-room angels and progress to our very own personal guardian angels, who serve as our protectors.

four
_____

Angels in the
Kingdom of God

For he has rescued us from the dominion of darkness and brought us into the Kingdom of the Son he loves.

Colossians 1:13

Every day, Jesus demonstrated and proclaimed the arrival of God's Kingdom on earth. His mission could be divided into three streams:

1. Preaching and teaching the Gospel
2. Healing the sick
3. Freeing people from evil

Isaiah's prophetic word concerning the coming Messiah was fulfilled in Jesus:

The Spirit of the Lord is on me,
because he [God] has anointed me
to preach good news to the poor.
He has sent me to proclaim freedom for the prisoners
and recovery of sight for the blind,
to release the oppressed,
to proclaim the year of the Lord's favor.

Luke 4:18–19

When Jesus boldly claimed, "Today this scripture is fulfilled in your hearing," He confirmed that the Kingdom of God, the time for God's salvation and His rule and reign, had arrived (Luke 4:21). From the very beginning of Jesus' Spirit-anointed ministry, bystanders from all walks of life marveled not only at His authoritative teaching (see Mark 1:22), but at the miracles He performed.

Today our Lord's ministry, with this same authority and power, continues through His followers, who are assisted by His holy angels. These three streams of ministry—announcing the Good News and bringing healing and deliverance—expand the Church throughout the world and usher in God's Kingdom. Angels are essential in ushering in the Kingdom. Their dwelling place is in the heavens, but their ministry under God's direction takes place throughout the earth. They are mighty, wise servants of God who faithfully protect those in need and bring healing and deliverance.

The following story reveals a mighty angel sent to encourage a congregation. This angel's appearance in a dramatic dream carried the message of the reign of the Kingdom of God. The angel also conveyed strength through his touch and warmth through his fiery eyes, both powerful reminders of the rule and reign of God.

An Angel Guarding a Church

I had a dream about an elegantly dressed woman, much like Audrey Hepburn, dressed in black and wearing large pearls, greeting me at the door to our church. We have no female ushers, so I thought it unusual that she was assisting that day. As she welcomed me in, she said she had someone for me to meet. As we walked down the aisle toward the front, I could sense there was a golden-haired "man" standing in the third row.

The man turned to look at me before we got there, and I noticed that he was a full two to three heads taller than anyone else. He stood up and took my hand into his, but with his palm up and hand flat. He looked at me intensely, and I could see fire dancing in his eyes. He spoke in this low, thundering voice and said, "The Lord reigns." I could feel something warm shoot into my hand and body. I turned away and then back, and he now had wings over wings—three sets on each side of his back. I knew clearly that he was the angel of our church, sent to remind us that the Lord reigns.

—Robin Morrison

Here are two more stories about angels at work in the churches. In the first, three angels minister to a congregation by guarding and helping the pastor. In the second, a young boy sees angels present at a service in an unusual way.

Angels Bring a Supernatural Anointing

Years ago, my husband and I were members of a Methodist church. The pastor was an exceptional pulpit preacher, one of those radiant messengers whose sermons manage to nurture the minds, hearts and spirits of those who gather to listen. I had always felt called to keep our clergy in my prayers. As the service began on this particular Sunday, I bowed my head to intercede on their behalf. My prayer time began, and the familiar sounds of a settling congregation drifted further into the background.

To my astonishment, I began to experience what I can only describe as seeing into the spiritual realm. What I "saw" was Jesus, silent and beautiful, entering the church's right side door. Following rapidly behind Him were three angels. In one moment they appeared at the doorway, and in the next, they moved across the church to where the preacher was standing. He was at the pulpit, preparing to start the service.

Two of the angels stopped and stood on either side of the preacher, while the third one approached and gently placed a burning coal in his mouth. Great excitement rose in my spirit as I knew there would be a supernatural anointing on all that he was about to say. I thanked God for this incredible gift to our church.

A great blessing washed over our congregation that morning—the sermon was alive with the unmistakable power of the Holy Spirit. After seeing those angels at work in my own church, I have to wonder how often they must quietly come alongside us to help, encourage and anoint us throughout our lives.

—Anonymous

Angels Enjoying a Service

One Sunday while in church, my son was smiling and chuckling as he gazed up at the ceiling. I worried that he was disrupting the service, so I leaned over and pulled him onto my lap, whispering, "You need to stop giggling. What's so funny?"

He replied, "The angels are so funny sitting up on the fans. See them? They are playing with each other as the fans turn."

I did not see anything when I looked up, but I could tell that he was really seeing something up there.

—Anonymous

Have you ever been in a situation where you felt someone was with you, but there was no one present? Or suddenly, you felt a hand on your shoulder and turned around to look, only to find no one there? Who is that in such situations? These are instances of God's holy angels coming to you and carrying strength and a message of God's love. That was the case for the seminarian in the next story.

An Angel Brings a Message of Security

While I was in seminary, I was eating lunch alone at a local restaurant. Feeling insecure about my studies and my ministry, I was talking silently to the Lord about it.

While I was waiting for my food, I saw a man wearing jeans and a white T-shirt. I looked a second time, possibly because he was so muscular and quite handsome. He walked by my table, and I read the word Security *written across the front of his shirt.*

It occurred to me that he might be a security guard somewhere, although I had never seen a uniform like his. I turned around to see if the name of his company might be written on the back of the shirt, but he was gone. There was no place for him to go in those few seconds that he was out of my line of vision. God had sent an angel to give me the message that I have security in Him.

—Anonymous

Angels also advance God's Kingdom under the direction of the Holy Spirit by engaging in spiritual warfare with the enemy. They carry messages and prayers, participate in healings, execute God's justice and guard and protect God's children. Angels have many roles and purposes in our lives, in the life of the Church and in the Kingdom.

Angelic Activity on the Increase

During seasons of increased angelic (and sometimes demonic) activity, my dog will sit during worship, ministry and prayer times and stare at the front door, wagging his tail as if he hears someone familiar coming onto our porch. He only behaves like this with close friends and family, when he can hear or see them outside, so I have checked several times to see if someone is there.

My dog also has growled deeply and protectively when there is demonic activity going on outside of the house.

—Anonymous

Their primary role is to advance the Kingdom through loyal service to God:

> The LORD has established his throne in heaven and his kingdom rules over all. Praise the LORD, you his angels, you mighty ones who do his bidding, who obey his word. Praise the LORD, all his heavenly hosts, you his servants who do his will.
>
> Psalm 103:19–21

Pure love motivates angels to serve God and advance His Kingdom. Often, unseen angels faithfully carry out their mission to reclaim God's creation, His children and His universe from enemy influence.

At the end of the age, mighty angels will become more active in the final work of the Kingdom.

> The harvest is the end of the age, and the harvesters are angels. The Son of Man will send out his angels, and they will weed out of his Kingdom everything that causes sin and all who do evil.
>
> Matthew 13:39–41

God has assigned His holy angels to eliminate sin and evil in preparation for the return of His Son, Jesus. "When the Son of Man comes in his glory, and all the angels with him, he will sit on his throne in heavenly glory" (Matthew 25:31). We are offered this overwhelming image of Jesus, the Son of God, taking His place on His throne, surrounded by the entire heavenly host.

"Then the end will come, when he [Jesus] hands over the kingdom to God the Father after he has destroyed all dominion, authority and power" (1 Corinthians 15:24). Jesus,

Angels on Guard

While driving home over a bridge, I looked up at the steeple of a church and saw two huge angels. They were very tall, with large wings, and they were standing on each side of the steeple. As I approached the next church, I saw angels there, too, but they looked different. I asked myself if they were just visiting, or if they were there all the time, like guardians. It came to me that they were there to guard.

Later on, I saw a similar angel, but smaller, on an Episcopal church near a university chapel across the bridge. Yet another time, taking a flight out of Washington, D.C., I saw a group of angels swarming far below the airplane, near the Capitol. I have not seen them since then.

—Anonymous

assisted by the holy angels, will have destroyed the enemies of the Kingdom of God.

> The seventh angel sounded his trumpet, and there were loud voices in heaven, which said: "The kingdom of the world has become the kingdom of our Lord and of his Christ, and he will reign for ever and ever."
>
> Revelation 11:15

If you want to enter God's Kingdom, I have included this prayer you can pray alone or with someone, trusting that Jesus will joyfully welcome you into His Kingdom:

Heavenly Father, I want to give my life to You and enter into Your Kingdom. I know that I have sinned, and I ask You to forgive me of all my sins, the ones I know about and the ones I don't know about. I believe that Jesus Christ is Your Son, the Son of God, and I believe that He died for my sins. I believe that You raised Him from the dead.

I ask You, Jesus Christ, to come into my heart. By the power of the Holy Spirit, transform me into the person You intended me to be from the moment of my conception. Thank You for dying for me and for giving me the gift of eternal life in Your Kingdom.

Thank you, Lord Jesus. Amen.

five

The Classification
of Angels

I saw an angel close by me, on my left side, in bodily form.
This I am not accustomed to see, unless very rarely. Though
I have visions of angels frequently, yet I see them only by an
intellectual vision. It was our Lord's will that in this vision I
should see the angel in this way. He was not large, but small
of stature, and most beautiful—his face burning, as if he were
one of the highest angels, who seem to be all of fire: they must
be those whom we call Cherubim. Their names they never tell
me; but I am aware that there is in heaven so great a differ-
ence between one angel and another, that I cannot explain it.[1]

—Saint Teresa of Avila

*A*fter years of being involved in ministry and studying the angelic realm, I have come to the conclu-
sion that the heavenly host consists of endless numbers of

angels who belong to differing ranks. Also differing are their power, glory, authority and purpose. Early Christian writers referred to "nine choirs of angels," an idea that reflects a complex system of angels created and organized by God. In my understanding, each office within the nine orders represents a different level of power, a different level of wisdom, a different rank and a different level of access to God. We can compare these ranks and orders to a governmental system. The apostle Paul wrote that both the visible and the invisible things in heaven and on earth were created by and for God, whether thrones or powers or rulers or authorities (see Colossians 1:16). We are told by Peter that Jesus Christ is in heaven at God's right hand—with angels, authorities and powers who are in submission to Him (see 1 Peter 3:22). Both Peter and Paul seem to indicate that there are orders of angelic beings ranking in power and position, all of them subject to Jesus Christ.

Nine Orders of Angels

In A.D. 500, the Christian theologian and philosopher Pseudo-Dionysius the Areopagite wrote about nine orders of angels[2] and taught that they were divided into three distinct ranks. Within these ranks power is distributed in descending order, with the higher-ranking angels possessing more power, more wisdom and greater access to God. The first order consists of *seraphim, cherubim* and *thrones.* The second order contains *dominions, powers* and *authorities* (or *virtues*). The third is composed of *principalities, archangels* and *angels.* Each order has its uniquely assigned service to God, and therefore each has separate responsibilities.

Thomas Aquinas, in his *Summa Theologica*, also wrote an entire section on angels and ranked them according to the Dionysian hierarchy. He assigned each rank a specific relationship to God, to the cosmos and to humans. He stated that the first rank, the seraphim, cherubim and thrones, all have direct contact with God and surround His throne. The angels in this first rank remain in His presence, constantly praising and worshiping Him. The second rank or tier, the dominions, powers and authorities, is comprised of angels assigned to the care of the physical universe or cosmos. The third order, the principalities, archangels and angels, is directly involved in human affairs. Principalities watch over and protect entire nations and geographical areas. Archangels are assigned to oversee angels and humans. Angels are given the task of the guardianship of individuals and churches.

Seraphim Angels

The name seraphim comes from the Hebrew word *seraph*, meaning "burning ones." They are on fire with the love of God, hence their name. In the Song of Solomon, love is described as "a blazing fire, like a mighty flame" (Song of Solomon 8:6). Many authors refer to the seraphim as the "radiant ones" because of the light reflecting off them. This light reflects God's light and presence. Characterized by their adoration of God, they are reported to be beautiful beyond imagination and noble in their appearance.

The seraphim manifest the glory of God by remaining forever in His radiant presence. Their position as the highest order in the angelic realm permits them complete access to the depths of God's love, to the very core of His heart, which is pure love. Try to imagine being in the deepest heart of pure love. What kind of transformation would occur in you? Most of us spend our entire lives just trying to discover God's love.

Isaiah experienced a dramatic vision when God called him as a prophet. In the vision, he was granted a glimpse into the throne room of God, where the angelic seraphim were attending God. They worship God continuously from above His throne, leading all of heaven in worship:

> In the year that King Uzziah died, I saw the Lord seated on a throne, high and exalted, and the train of his robe filled the temple. Above him were seraphs, each with six wings: With two wings they covered their faces, with two they covered their feet, and with two they were flying. And they were calling to one another:
>
>> "Holy, holy, holy is the LORD Almighty;
>> the whole earth is full of his glory."
>
> At the sound of their voices the doorposts and thresholds shook and the temple was filled with smoke.
>
> "Woe to me!" I cried. "I am ruined! For I am a man of unclean lips, and I live among a people of unclean lips, and my eyes have seen the King, the LORD Almighty."
>
> Then one of the seraphs flew to me with a live coal in his hand, which he had taken with tongs from the altar. With it he touched my mouth and said, "See, this has touched your lips; your guilt is taken away and your sin atoned for."
>
> Isaiah 6:1–7

This angelic interchange is an extraordinary example of the complete love the seraphim have for God and His children. Much like us, Isaiah did not feel worthy enough or holy enough to respond to the call of God. When God calls us to serve Him in a special way or vocation, we need to remember that our Lord Jesus always provides a way of purification. The angel cleansed, encouraged and strengthened Isaiah. After the angel's touch, Isaiah responded immediately to God's call by saying, "Here I am. Send me!" (Isaiah 6:8).

We study Scripture and read Christian books. We pray, come to church, attend conferences and feel blessed if we have a few intimate connections with God over the course of a lifetime. Yet many people who have been Christians for years have confided in me that they have never experienced God's loving presence. If we want to enter into His "heart of love," we need heaven's help. The angels provide that help, lifting our hearts and prayers to God.

Cherubim Angels

The cherubim constitute the second order of angels in the angelic hierarchy. These mighty angels are called the guardians of the throne of God. Like the seraphim, they stay in the heavenly throne room, worshiping and guarding God. Christian tradition tells us they are beautiful beyond description. Ezekiel's detailed description of the cherubim portrays majestic beings of great beauty, strength and power:

> I looked, and I saw a windstorm coming out of the north—an immense cloud with flashing lightning and surrounded by brilliant light. The center of the fire looked like glowing metal, and in the fire was what looked like four living creatures. In appearance their form was that of a man, but each of them had four faces and four wings.
>
> Ezekiel 1:4–6

Ezekiel identifies these beings as cherubim (see Ezekiel 10:15 17).

Cherubim first appear in the Garden of Eden account. After God banished Adam and Eve from the Garden, He "placed on the east side of the Garden of Eden cherubim and a flaming sword flashing back and forth to guard the way to the tree of life" (Genesis 3:24).

The etymology of the word *cherubim* is not easy to ascertain, though it has been suggested that it means "to cover" or "to guard." In Scripture, God directs the building of the Ark of the Covenant (see Exodus 25:18–22; 37:6–9). It had wood overlaid with figures of golden cherubim guarding the mercy seat. Cherubim are also mentioned when God directed expert craftsmen to place images of cherubim on the inner curtains and the veil of the Tabernacle (see Exodus 26:1, 31). God also directed that the cherubim's images be carved into the doors of Solomon's Temple (see 1 Kings 6:32–35).

References in the book of Psalms state that God dwells between the cherubim (see Psalms 80:1; 99:1). From this vantage point, the cherubim worship God and shield His glory. A few ancient texts refer to them as burning with love for God, much like the seraphim. King David sang, "He parted the heavens and came down; dark clouds were under his feet. He mounted the cherubim and flew; he soared on the wings of the wind" (2 Samuel 22:10–11).

Thrones

Thrones are placed third in the first rank or triad. Thrones are often referred to as pure spirits of contemplation and intellect. According to Thomas Aquinas, thrones have a more perfect nature and keener intelligence, mercy and justice than the lesser angels.

The highest triad of angels (seraphim, cherubim and thrones) comprises the heavenly council where God presides (see Psalm 82:1). Since all wisdom originates in God, these angels understand God's will and direct the lower angels accordingly. King David makes reference to this assembly or council of holy ones:

> The heavens praise your wonders, O LORD, your faithfulness too, in the assembly of the holy ones. For who in the skies above can compare with the LORD? Who is like the LORD among the heavenly beings? In the council of the holy ones God is greatly feared; he is more awesome than all who surround him.
>
> Psalm 89:5–7

David's vision is that of a great assembly of angels in heaven attending to God by serving Him.

Daniel also had a vision of a similar scene in heaven. He said that as he looked on,

> thrones were set in place,
>   and the Ancient of Days took his seat.
> His clothing was as white as snow;
>   the hair of his head was white like wool.
> His throne was flaming with fire,
>   and its wheels were all ablaze.
> A river of fire was flowing,
>   coming out from before him.
> Thousands upon thousands attended him;
>   ten thousand times ten thousand stood before him.
>
> Daniel 7:9–10

These visions transcend our ability to imagine the magnitude of God's awesome presence in heaven. Like David and Daniel, we try to open the eyes of our hearts and explore the depths of His fierce love for us (see Ephesians 1:18). Recognizing that we cannot reach this realm until we live fully in God's presence, we rely on the angels to impart God's love to us.

John, while exiled on the island of Patmos, beheld a vision of heaven's throne room:

> At once I was in the Spirit, and there before me was a throne in heaven with someone sitting on it. And the one who sat there had the appearance of jasper and carnelian. A rainbow, resembling an emerald, encircled the throne. . . . From the throne came flashes of lightning, rumblings and peals of thunder.
>
> Revelation 4:2–3, 5

Paul's description of God seated on His throne portrays the "unapproachable light" in which God dwells (1 Timothy 6:16). God is the source of all light. Several scriptural visions of heaven use the imagery of brilliant jewels or precious metals such as gold. God is compared to the reflected brilliance emanating from the jewels and radiating light above His head. Matthew's gospel account of Jesus' transfiguration on Mount Tabor says that when Jesus was transfigured, "His face shone like the sun, and his clothes became as white as the light" (Matthew 17:2). We begin to understand why the seraphim, cherubim and thrones are filled with fire and brilliant light. They, like the jewels, reflect God's brilliant countenance.

Dominion Angels

Thomas Aquinas referred to the second rank or tier of angels as "angels of the cosmos or universe." Dominions, powers and authorities (or virtues) comprise this level. Traditionally, these are referred to as "angels of the world order." Power, wisdom and judgment are attributes of these angels, equipping them to carry out their mission.

Dominion angels focus on the execution of God's judgments and on regulating the duties of lower angels. The two angels who appeared in Sodom to warn Lot and his family of the city's impending destruction are considered dominion angels. They told Lot, "Get them [your family] out of here, because we are going to destroy this place. The outcry to the LORD against his people is so great that he has sent us to destroy it" (Genesis 19:12–13). In this Scripture, dominion angels are carrying out God's judgments. These majestic angels regulate the order of God's universe by overseeing galaxies, stars and the earth. They are also sent to leaders to impart God's wisdom.

Power Angels

The second group in this rank is comprised of power angels, God's warrior angels who are constantly engaged in the age-old battle with the evil forces of our unseen universe. Paul wrote to the Ephesian church about this unseen spiritual battle:

> Our struggle is not against flesh and blood, but against the rulers, against the authorities, against the powers of this dark world and against the spiritual forces of evil in the heavenly realms.
>
> Ephesians 6:12

As Paul describes these fallen angels of Satan, who carry the same names as holy angels, he warns us not only to be aware of these evil forces, but to act by putting on the full armor of God to protect ourselves. As we battle against these evil forces, we have the authority of Jesus Christ and the power of the Holy Spirit.

This struggle with evil is often overlooked by many church leaders. Non-Western cultures seem to have a better understanding of this evil war than we do. As we engage in this spiritual battle to advance God's Kingdom, the dominion angels are constantly battling evil in the unseen realm. Dominion angels also govern angels in the lower order who are engaged in spiritual warfare.

Authorities or Virtues

Authorities or virtues are mighty angels sent from God who bestow miracle-working graces on the earth. They are also involved in helping to maintain order in the earth. The Holy Spirit empowers them to directly affect the natural world order. We have a glimpse of their influence in the story where Jesus stilled the raging storm:

> Then he got into the boat and his disciples followed him. Without warning, a furious storm came up on the lake, so that the waves swept over the boat. But Jesus was sleeping. The disciples went and woke him, saying, "Lord, save us! We're going to drown!"
>
> He replied, "You of little faith, why are you so afraid?" Then he got up and rebuked the winds and the waves, and it was completely calm.

The men were amazed and asked, "What kind of man is this? Even the winds and the waves obey him!"

Matthew 8:23–27

The Sea of Galilee is a unique lake thirteen miles long and seven miles wide. Because winds can intensify over the lake, sudden violent storms appear unexpectedly, with large waves. Many of Jesus' disciples were expert fishermen from that region. In the full face of this fierce storm, their fears were justified. Remarkably, Jesus was found sleeping during the peak of the storm, which shows both His faith and His fatigue. The disciples were amazed that Jesus had authority over the howling winds and the towering waves. In Israel, many false messiahs had appeared in the years before Jesus, some able to perform healings, but none before had control over nature or had the power to raise the dead. In exercising His authority over nature, Jesus shocked His disciples, but this miracle contributed to their growing realization that this Jesus must be more than a mere man. Did the angels calm the storm at His command? We are not sure, but this influence over nature has traditionally been ascribed to angels.

Virtue angels bestow remarkable graces from God to work great miracles on the earth and in the heavenlies. They especially impart miracle-working grace to God's people in times of need.

Principality Angels

Principalities form the order of angels directly involved in human affairs. They, along with archangels and angels, make up the third rank or tier in the hierarchy, and they oversee groups and individuals to provide protection, guidance and healing. Some are consistently present to us (our guardian angels are good examples), or they come in response to our prayers in times of need. Though often undetected, their holy presence brings us the courage, strength and grace we need for our earthly journey.

Angels and humans share a close bond arranged by God. Jacob's dream of the ladder with the angels on it portrays this angelic connection between heaven and earth. Jacob "had a dream in which he saw a stairway resting on the earth, with its top reaching to heaven, and the angels of God were ascending and descending on it." Jacob's response was, "This is the gate of heaven" (Genesis 28:12, 17). This imagery showed Jacob the intimate connection of the visible to the invisible world.

When Jesus called Nathaniel as a disciple, He said, "I tell you the truth, you shall see heaven open, and the angels of God ascending and descending on the Son of Man" (John 1:51). Jesus shared this image of the ladder between earth and heaven in order to stress angelic roles as intermediaries between God and people. Of course, the ladder is not necessary for angels, but the image assures us that we are connected to the angelic host of heaven.

Principalities are mighty angels of greater wisdom, power and authority than we can imagine. Their energy is concentrated on directing the archangels and guardian angels as they protect the children of God and the Church. They also constantly battle the enemies of God by encouraging and strengthening the angels under their command.

During our Lord's time on earth, principalities guarded and strengthened Him when He fasted for forty days in the wilderness. These principality angels also guarded Him during His Passion in the Garden of Gethsemane and then in

His final hours during the crucifixion. Jesus received strength from the ministry of angels, which enabled Him to endure His intense sufferings. He was aware of their attentive presence surrounding Him, and He knew they were ready with their full force to rescue Him, if only He would call on them. He did not, however, permit them to rescue Him from His path to the cross. How can we begin to imagine their agony as they watched Jesus, their beloved master, being nailed to a cross and suffering indescribable pain as He carried the weight of mankind's sin? The angels remained on the sidelines during this final battle against their enemy, called as witnesses to the greatest sacrifice ever offered.

In the Garden of Gethsemane, remember how Jesus warned the arresting officers about the army of angels at His disposal? He remarked, "Do you think I cannot call on my Father, and he will at once put at my disposal more than twelve legions of angels?" (Matthew 26:53). Jesus used the word *legion*, a Roman military term, indicating that twelve legions, or 72,000 angels, stood by to intervene, if He so desired. The angels must have felt their hearts wrench when they heard Jesus' words refusing their assistance. Their devotion and obedience to the will of the Father held them in place.

Archangels

Archangels make up the next order. "For the Lord himself will come down from heaven, with a loud command, with the voice of the archangel and with the trumpet call of God" (1 Thessalonians 4:16). Archangels are often referred to as the "Angels of the Presence." The prefix "arch" signifies a higher-ranking angel who is over a group of angels. According to tradition, there are seven archangels, but only three are named in Scripture. The names of the seven are a matter of debate, but we know three of them—Michael, Gabriel and Raphael.

In the Intertestamental period—the four hundred years between the writing of the Old and New Testament books, all which we know today as the canonized Bible—other books were written by rabbis of the Jewish faith. In these books such as Judith, Tobit and Enoch, we find references to angels (for example, the archangel Raphael in the book of Tobit). These books are not acknowledged as part of the canon, but they are recognized as scholarly literature written by devout rabbis and can be found in what is known as the Apocrypha.

The canonized Bible does not mention Raphael by name, but we glean from the apocryphal book of Tobit (12:15) that he is "one of the seven angels . . . who stand ever ready to enter the presence of the glory of the Lord." And seven archangels are listed in the apocryphal book of Enoch (40:8–9):

> After this I besought the angel of peace, who proceeded with me, to explain all that was concealed. I said to him, "Who are those whom I have seen on the four sides, and whose words I have heard and written down?" He replied, "The first is the merciful, the patient, the holy Michael. The second is he who presides over every suffering and every affliction of the sons of men, the holy Raphael. The third, who presides over all that is powerful, is Gabriel. And the fourth, who presides over repentance, and the hope of those who will inherit eternal life, is Phanuel." These are the four angels of the most high God, and their four voices, which at that time I heard.

The number of archangels differs according to the source. Pseudo-Dionysius lists the seven archangels as Michael,

Gabriel, Raphael, Uriel, Chamuel, Jophiel and Zadiel.[3] Let's take a look at the scriptural sources, though, that list three of them.

The Archangel Michael

Scripture identifies Michael, whose name means "one who is like God," as an archangel. "Even the archangel Michael, when he was disputing with the devil about the body of Moses, did not himself dare to condemn him for slander but said, 'The Lord rebuke you!'" (Jude 1:9).

This dispute over Moses' body sheds light on the relationship between Michael, referred to as one of the princes of heaven (see Daniel 10:13), and Lucifer, or Satan, the prince of darkness. Michael, who according to tradition will cast Satan into hell, is obviously withholding his might until God gives the command to destroy Satan and his demons. This historic conflict between Satan and Michael stems from the time of the great rebellion in heaven, in which Lucifer, previously a cherub in the courts of heaven, was cast out of God's Kingdom, along with the third of the angelic realm who rebelled with him:

> And there was war in heaven. Michael and his angels fought against the dragon [Lucifer], and the dragon and his angels fought back. But he was not strong enough, and they lost their place in heaven. The great dragon was hurled down—that ancient serpent called the devil, or Satan, who leads the whole world astray. He was hurled to the earth, and his angels with him.
>
> Revelation 12:7–9

Jesus makes reference to Satan's fall in the gospel of Luke, following the return of the 72 disciples. Jesus said,

> I saw Satan fall like lightning from heaven. I have given you authority to trample on snakes and scorpions and to overcome all the power of the enemy; nothing will harm you.
>
> Luke 10:18–19

His followers were overjoyed that "even the demons submit to us in your name" (verse 17).

In the book of Daniel, Michael is called the prince of God's chosen people (Israel): "At that time Michael, the great prince who protects your people, will arise" (Daniel 12:1). In the New Testament, Michael continues in this role as the protector of God's New Covenant children. In art Michael is usually depicted as a strong young warrior. He bears a shield, armor and a sword or lance and is often portrayed crushing Satan underfoot. In John's account of the end of time, Jesus returns to earth accompanied by Michael and his angels, and Satan is cast into the pit of hell (see Revelation 19:20).

In 1886 Pope Leo XIII added a special prayer to Michael for Catholics to say at the end of every Mass: "Saint Michael the Archangel, defend us in battle. Be our protection against the wickedness and snares of the devil . . ."[4] This prayer was dropped from the liturgy in 1964. But Pope John Paul II, who performed several exorcisms in his lifetime, felt the need to create a new prayer to aid Catholics in their spiritual battle, and he referred back to Pope Leo XIII's prayer to Saint Michael: "May prayer strengthen us for the spiritual battle that the letter to the Ephesians speaks of: 'Be strong in the Lord and in the strength of his might (Ephesians 6:10).'"[5]

The image of Michael that emerges is a mighty warrior angel noted for his great courage, wisdom and might. He is also portrayed as a general in charge of countless legions of angels endlessly engaged in a fierce battle with Satan and his demons. This battle will continue until the end of this earth as we know it.

What follows is my story of an amazing encounter with an archangel.

An Encounter with an Archangel

Following my return to the United States from several years in the Middle East, I established Christian Counseling Services in Clearwater, Florida. Most of my clients were Christians who needed counseling for moderate mood disorders. Occasionally, someone would come seeking healing prayer after a crisis or trauma.

One day as I arrived at work, my office manager, Libby, cautioned me about a client waiting in my office. Libby described him as "spiritually dark." (She had a way of seeing spiritual light and darkness.) Unfortunately I brushed her comment aside, distracted by other problems.

Entering my office, I immediately knew I should have paid more attention to Libby's discernment. The client who sat opposite me was by far the most disturbing person I have ever counseled. I should say here that my therapeutic work before I went into private practice was in psychiatric hospitals and had included murderers, serial killers and rapists, many of whom carried great darkness. But this darkness was on a totally different level. At once I experienced chills, an increased pulse rate, nausea and an intense headache. I knew I was in the presence of an extraordinarily powerful and evil being. Everything within me was on full alert.

I do not believe anything has ever disturbed me as much as this strange man sitting quietly before me. I wanted to get away from the intense darkness he carried. Even my "angel fish" in the fish tank swam to the opposite side of the tank in an attempt to hide. The sound of the ticking clock seemed loud and intense, as though time had slowed down.

I prayed under my breath for God's help. After a few moments (which felt like an eternity), I cautiously began the interview with the standard questions, "Why are you here? What is your problem?"

The man calmly replied, "I don't have a problem— you do."

Unsure how to proceed after his comment, I asked why he made the appointment if he did not have a problem. Again, I experienced that eerie silence.

Finally, the man said, "You have come to our attention because of the work you are doing to help people. I am a warlock in Satan's service, and I have been sent to stop you."

Nothing in my training as a psychotherapist had prepared me for this situation. Quickly flipping through my limited understanding of the realm of witches and warlocks, I remembered that warlocks were reputed to have mystical powers given by Satan. They supposedly functioned at a higher level in the realm of evil than most other members of satanic covens.

Several questions flashed through my mind. Is he psychotic? Is he seriously deluded? Does he have grandiose delusions of power? Aside from his bizarre statements, he appeared somewhat normal. He proceeded, however, to tell me stories of his ability to kill people without even touching them by "using the powers of Satan."

At this point, I was trying to decide what action I could take to defuse the situation. I excused myself from the session to get a cup of coffee, though I didn't really need the caffeine. I simply needed to step out to pray for help and direction.

Libby, my discerning office manager, took one look at my face and immediately knew I was disturbed. She quickly told me that God had already revealed to her who this man was, as well as his assignment against me. She told me to return to the session, assuring me that God had already taken care of the situation.

When I returned to my office, I knew within my heart that this servant of Satan held no power over God or me. As John said, "You, dear children, are from God and have overcome them, because the one who is in you is greater than the one who is in the world" (1 John 4:4). The man began to threaten me again, but my fear was gone. I looked directly into his dark eyes and said, "I am not afraid of you. The one I serve is far greater than your master, and God and His holy angels protect me." Immediately I felt courageous, so I continued to assert God's strong protection and to

speak of the cross of Christ and His victory over evil.
Moments after speaking those words, a comforting
presence flooded the room, and I became aware of a
majestic and holy presence beside me.

Suddenly the warlock looked beyond me to my
right side. A look of terror came over his face as he
screamed in fear, leapt out of his chair and ran out
of the office, past Libby and down several flights of
stairs without waiting for the elevator. I never saw
him again.

I have reflected on this experience many times since that day. Several truths emerge. First, when you are actively involved in the Kingdom ministry of bringing healing and freedom to suffering souls, you will come to the attention of the enemy, who will want to stop you. Second, the protection of our Lord and His holy angels covers us in the battle, "For he will command his angels concerning you to guard you in all your ways" (Psalm 91:11). We need to ask God to send His angels to protect and defend us.

I believe that God sent Michael the archangel that day to defend me in battle against the powers of darkness sent against me. I also believe the warlock was "seeing" into the spiritual realm and saw Michael, the mighty warrior of God, prepared for battle. Since that day, I have completely trusted in the strong protection of God's angels. I have also learned to pay attention when a discerning Christian gives me a warning.

The Archangel Gabriel

Gabriel is the name of the mighty archangel who stands "in the presence of God" (Luke 1:19). His name means "mighty one of God" or "God is my strength." Gabriel is the Lord's chief messenger, overseeing and commanding countless messenger angels. He is named four times in the Bible. During each biblical appearance, Gabriel brings an important message to someone. His recipients include Daniel, Zechariah (John the Baptist's father) and Mary, the mother of Jesus. We can also assume that Gabriel was the angel who appeared to Joseph, Mary's husband, in his dreams to warn him about Herod's intention of killing Jesus.

Gabriel is portrayed as a high-ranking archangel possessing great might and wisdom. He is the bearer of good news, always revealing God's mercy and love to those chosen by God. In Gabriel's first appearance in Scripture, he delivers the interpretation of a vision concerning Israel's future to the prophet Daniel. "While I, Daniel, was watching the vision and trying to understand it, there before me stood one who looked like a man. And I heard a man's voice from the Ulai [River] calling, 'Gabriel, tell this man the meaning of the vision'" (Daniel 8:15–16).

Whose voice directed Gabriel to interpret the vision for Daniel? Gabriel appeared to be following a command given by a higher-order angel who was communicating the meaning of the vision. Gabriel then revealed the meaning to Daniel after he touched Daniel and raised him to his feet (see verse 18). Most, if not all, angelic appearances in the Bible seem to happen during visions of future events.

Later, Daniel recorded that while he was still praying,

> Gabriel, the man I had seen in the earlier vision, came to me in swift flight. . . . He instructed me and said to me, "Daniel, I have now come to give you insight and understanding."
>
> Daniel 9:21–22

Here we have the prince of the messenger angels, Gabriel, visiting Daniel on two separate occasions to give him God's direction and strength. In both these visions, Gabriel assumes a human appearance. In a later chapter, however, Gabriel appears in an altogether different guise, in his spiritual form, and only Daniel, but not those with him, could see Gabriel:

> I looked up and there before me was a man dressed in linen, with a belt of the finest gold around his waist. His body was like chrysolite [a translucent, semiprecious stone], his face like lightning, his eyes like flaming torches, his arms and legs like the gleam of burnished bronze, and his voice like the sound of a multitude.
>
> Daniel 10:5–6

Try to imagine your own response to this awesome vision of Gabriel. Perhaps you will begin to understand Daniel's overwhelming fear, which caused him to faint. However, Gabriel's loving care toward Daniel is evident. Daniel recorded,

> A hand touched me and set me trembling on my hands and knees. He [Gabriel] said, "Daniel, you who are highly esteemed, consider carefully the words I am about to speak to you, and stand up, for I have now been sent to you."
>
> Daniel 10:10–11

It is difficult to imagine what our response would be if a mighty archangel appeared and told us that we were highly esteemed by God. Those words carry the power to restore purpose and life. Angels seem to be in awe of how much God loves humanity. Gabriel told Daniel again, "Do not be afraid, O man highly esteemed . . . Peace! Be strong now;

be strong." And Daniel said, "When he spoke to me, I was strengthened" (Daniel 10:19). One of the great roles of angels is to strengthen and encourage us when we feel discouraged by life's challenges. The angels strengthened Jesus when He was weak. Remember, the angelic hosts of heaven stand ready to help you in your journey.

Daniel chapter 10 also reveals the ongoing dynamic spiritual battle in the heavenlies between angels and demons. These demonic forces attempt to thwart the mission of the angels. Gabriel, whom God sent with the meaning of the vision, was delayed for three weeks by a demon. Daniel faithfully continued to fast and pray for the three-week duration. Finally, the archangel Michael came to assist Gabriel in the battle. Together they overcame the evil spirit, allowing Gabriel to complete his mission. This insight into the unseen spiritual battle helps us understand that although the answer to our prayers may be hindered, we need to persevere as Daniel did, trusting that the holy angels will prevail.

The Archangel Gabriel and John the Baptist

Another dynamic story about Gabriel appears in the gospel of Luke, when Gabriel delivers a life-changing message to an elderly couple. Zechariah was a priest, and Elizabeth, his wife, was a relative of Mary, the mother of Jesus. "Both of them were upright in the sight of God" (Luke 1:6), but Elizabeth was unable to conceive a child. Their childless state caused them great shame in their culture. Due to their age, they had come to the realization that they would never have children. And then God stepped into their circumstances.

Zechariah was a priest in the Abijah division, which consisted of 1,000 priests. Altogether, Israel had 20,000 priests broken into 24 subgroups, all serving in the Temple on a rotating basis. Because of the great number of priests, a lottery system was used to see which priest would be chosen by God to enter the holy of holies and burn the ceremonial incense. Each morning, lots were cast to select the chosen priest. On this particular day, Zechariah was chosen. This selection could only happen once in a priest's lifetime, so the honor was enormous. When smoke from the incense (burned twice daily) rose toward heaven, the worshipers in the Temple prayed, believing that their prayers rose with the smoke to God.

A rabbi once told me that when a priest entered the holy of holies to pray and burn incense, a rope was tied around his ankle in case he was unable to come out for some unforeseen reason. If this happened, no one was allowed to go in to help him. I often wonder whether or not I would be willing to enter a sacred place where God "lived" if going in required tying a rope around my ankle. What about you?

While Zechariah was burning the incense at the altar, the assembled worshipers prayed outside. Suddenly, an angel of the Lord appeared just to the right of the altar of incense.

When Zechariah saw him, he was startled and was gripped with fear. But the angel said to him: "Do not be afraid, Zechariah; your prayer has been heard. Your wife Elizabeth will bear you a son, and you are to call him John. He will be a joy and delight to you, and many will rejoice because of his birth, for he will be great in the sight of the Lord. He is never to take wine or other fermented drink, and he will be filled with the Holy Spirit even before he is born. He will bring back many of the people of Israel to the Lord their God. And he will go on before the Lord, in the spirit and power of Elijah."

Luke 1:12–17

Zechariah was so overwhelmed with this seemingly impossible good news that he doubted the angel. He asked, "How can I be sure of this? I am an old man and my wife is well along in years" (verse 18).

Apparently, doubt was not the response Gabriel expected. He responded,

> I am Gabriel. I stand in the presence of God, and I have been sent to speak to you and to tell you this good news. And now you will be silent and not able to speak until the day this happens, because you did not believe my words, which will come true at their appointed time.
>
> verses 19–20

This story brings up several considerations:

1. Faith, not doubt, is expected when an angel brings a message from God.
2. God eventually answers our prayers. Zechariah and Elizabeth probably had prayed for a long time for a son, an heir, to remove their shame in being childless, and Gabriel said, "Your prayer has been heard" (Luke 1:13).
3. God is not limited by our human limitations—even our physical ones.
4. This prophetic word of Gabriel's became a reality. Jesus said of John the Baptist, "I tell you, among those born of women there is no one greater than John; yet the one who is least in the kingdom of God is greater than he" (Luke 7:28).
5. Angels do not struggle with their identity in God, as we do. Gabriel's response to Zechariah's doubt was to say, "I am Gabriel." Try that kind of response the next time

someone questions your place in God's Kingdom. He also said, "I stand in the presence of God" (Luke 1:19). In other words, "I know who I am, why I was created and who loves me."

6. Angels have the authority and power to make decisions and execute judgment "on the spot." Immediately Zechariah became mute until John was born and circumcised on the eighth day, just as the angel said.

After the birth of his son, Zechariah had his voice returned. He immediately began to praise God, and he delivered a profound prophetic word from the Holy Spirit:

> And you, my child, will be called a prophet of the
>   Most High;
>   for you will go on before the Lord to prepare the
>   way for him,
>   to give his people the knowledge of salvation
>   through the forgiveness of their sins,
>   because of the tender mercy of our God,
>   by which the rising sun will come to us from heaven
>   to shine on those living in darkness
>   and in the shadow of death,
>   to guide our feet into the path of peace.
>   Luke 1:76–79

God used Gabriel to bring this joyful news to Zechariah and Elizabeth, radically changing their personal lives and also the course of human history.

The Archangel Gabriel and the Virgin Mary

After blessing Zechariah and Elizabeth, Gabriel had another message to deliver, this time to a young virgin living in a tiny village named Nazareth in Galilee. Her name was Mary, and she was destined to bring forth the long-awaited Messiah, Jesus Christ. Again, an angel's announcement was the precursor to an event that forever changed the history of humanity.

The Archangel Raphael—Angel of Healing

In the apocryphal book of Tobit (12:14–15), Raphael is the archangel God sends to heal and guide Tobit's family during a time of great need: "God sent me to heal you [Tobit] and your daughter-in-law, Sarah. I am Raphael, one of the seven angels who stand ever ready to enter the presence of the glory of the Lord."

The name *Raphael* means "God heals." He is the archangel who oversees healing. This identification of Raphael as a healing angel has at least two other sources. One of them is in the apocryphal book of Enoch. Ancient Christian writers named Raphael as the mighty angel of God who healed the earth when it was defiled by the fallen angels following the great rebellion in heaven. The other source, however, is scriptural. In John's gospel, an angel of the Lord came and stirred the water to empower it for healing. Many consider this angel to be Raphael:

> Some time later, Jesus went up to Jerusalem for a feast of the Jews. Now there is in Jerusalem near the Sheep Gate a pool, which in Aramaic is called Bethesda and which is surrounded by five covered colonnades. Here a great number of disabled people used to lie—the blind, the lame, the paralyzed. One who was there had been an invalid for thirty-eight years. When Jesus saw him lying there and learned that he had

been in this condition for a long time, he asked him, "Do you want to get well?"

"Sir," the invalid replied, "I have no one to help me into the pool when the water is stirred. While I am trying to get in, someone else goes down ahead of me."

Then Jesus said to him, "Get up! Pick up your mat and walk." At once the man was cured; he picked up his mat and walked.

John 5:1–9

The amazing thing is that the New International Version (1984) above says the water was "stirred," with no mention of the angel. The King James Version very explicitly states that as a great multitude of the sick waited around the pool, "an angel went down at a certain time into the pool and stirred up the water; then whoever stepped in first, after the stirring of the water, was made well of whatever disease he had" (John 5:4). The angel received healing power from God and transferred it to the water, but it seems it was only enough to heal one person. The first one to enter the pool afterward was miraculously healed.

Guardian Angels

Guardian angels are the last order of angels in the angelic hierarchy. Christian tradition and Scripture confirm our belief in the reality of these celestial beings assigned to vigilantly protect individuals and groups. Jesus assumed this basic belief when He said, "See that you do not look down on one of these little ones. For I tell you that their angels in heaven always see the face of my Father in heaven" (Matthew 18:10). Apparently, a powerful guardian angel is assigned to each

Angels at a Baby's Birth

Many angels were present for the birth of my sister's baby. They seemed so happy and delighted. When her doctor came in the next day, I could see that he had an angel about three-quarters his size who followed him around everywhere.

—Anonymous

of us and remains with us throughout our lives on earth. At death, the angel guides us to our eternal home.

Recorded throughout Scripture are stories of angelic interventions in the lives of ordinary people. One of my favorite Bible stories as a child was about King Nebuchadnezzar and the three young Jewish subjects whom he commanded to be thrown into a fiery furnace. I still remember the song we sang in Sunday school about these faithful servants of God who refused to worship the idol the king had erected in place of God.

The place was Babylon, and King Nebuchadnezzar was attempting to unify religious worship. He created a golden idol and commanded his people to fall down and worship it or be thrown into a blazing furnace. The king flew into a rage when he was told that Shadrach, Meshach and Abednego refused. These three replied,

If we are thrown into the blazing furnace, the God we serve is able to save us from it, and he will rescue us from your hand, O king. But even if he does not, we want you to know, O king, that we will not serve your gods or worship the image of gold you have set up.

Daniel 3:17–18

Furious, the king ordered strong soldiers to bind the young men and throw them into the blazing fire. The fire shooting out of the furnace was so hot that the king's soldiers who threw them in were instantly killed. Gazing into the furnace, the king said, "Look! I see four men walking around in the fire, unbound and unharmed, and the fourth looks like a son of the gods" (verse 25).

The one the king saw who looked like a "son of the gods" was probably a radiant angel sent to protect God's children in the midst of the flames. This mighty angel in the furnace had the appearance of a god or someone "otherworldly." Guardian angels intervene in our daily struggles to shield us from danger and to accompany us through life's difficulties. When Shadrach, Meshach and Abednego emerged from the furnace, those around them "saw that the fire had not harmed their bodies, nor was a hair of their heads singed; their robes were not scorched, and there was no smell of fire on them" (verse 27). Only the ropes that bound them were burned.

God still sets captives free today. Have you ever felt bound and trapped? Forced into a situation that you did not choose? Innocent, but found guilty? Condemned without a trial? Imagine how these three young men felt. Read their response again when the king made his threats. Paraphrased, it reads, "God will save us from you, but even if He does not, we will not betray Him." Forced into this situation, they trusted God to save them or be with them in the fire. They had simple faith in the One they had come to trust. God sent an angel not only to be with them, but to deliver them. He can do the same for you.

A similar story concerns the great prophet Daniel, framed by jealous co-workers because he refused to follow King

Darius's order to stop praying to anyone but the king for thirty days. When Daniel continued praying to God daily, he was cast into a den of hungry lions. (The Persians would capture wild lions and keep them in deep caves to torture and kill anyone who conspired against the king.) After spending the entire night with the lions, Daniel emerged the following day without any wounds. When the king saw Daniel, he was overcome with joy because he secretly admired Daniel. "My God sent his angel, and he shut the mouths of the lions," Daniel told the king. "They have not hurt me, because I was found innocent in his sight" (Daniel 6:22).

Mighty angels defend God's innocent children. Did you ever wonder how this powerful angel and Daniel passed their time together? They were probably worshiping God for His faithfulness.

Several other Bible stories reveal angels busily guarding, rescuing and strengthening those in need. Some even cooked food for hungry prophets. Moses received his call from God to deliver the Hebrew children out of Egypt when an angel of the Lord appeared in a burning bush. Throughout an entire night, Jacob wrestled with a man whom some believe was an angel—or was it God directly? An angel fed and encouraged Elijah when he was fleeing from Jezebel. An angel reassured Hagar when she and her son, Ishmael, fled from their community into the desert. An angel stopped the hand of Abraham when he was about to sacrifice his beloved son Isaac. (See Exodus 3:2; Genesis 32:24; 1 Kings 19:5–7; Genesis 21:17; 22:11–18.)

The prophet Elisha, who inherited a double portion of Elijah's spirit, had a remarkable gift of revealing God's heart of mercy and compassion. When King Aram of Syria sent strong warriors with horses and chariots to surround Dothan, where Elisha was staying, fear struck the heart of Elisha's servant. What was Elisha's response? "Don't be afraid. . . . Those who are with us are more than those who are with them." Then Elisha prayed, "O LORD, open his eyes so he may see," and "the LORD opened the servant's eyes, and he looked and saw the hills full of horses and chariots of fire all around Elisha" (2 Kings 6:16–17).

In response to Elisha's prayer, his servant saw the mighty heavenly host ready to fight for God's prophet. At first, only Elisha could see them, until his servant's eyes were also opened through prayer. If only we had our eyes opened to see God's provision in times of great need.

When I moved to Jerusalem in 1974, the Yom Kippur War had just ended. Israel had fought against a coalition of Arab states led by Egypt and Syria. This coalition was trying to recapture previously held Arab territories that were lost to Israel during the Six-Day War of June 1967. The Yom Kippur War began with surprise attacks on the Golan Heights in northern Israel and in the Sinai at the southern boundary of Israel. These attacks were executed during the Feast of Yom Kippur, one of the holiest days in the Jewish faith. Many Jewish leaders, soldiers and civilians were praying in their synagogues at that time. While a few soldiers guarded their borders, swift, full-force invasions were carried out against Israel with the element of surprise. Stories were told of Israeli soldiers rushing to their command posts still wearing their prayer shawls. Everything looked bleak and hopeless. But then, God gave the command to His angelic warriors.

During my first days in Israel, I noticed several cars that featured bumper stickers stating, "God still fights Israel's battles!" I asked the drivers about this message, and the answers were all similar. When the surprise attacks occurred, the Jewish soldiers and equipment could not get to their posts on time, and yet, all along the borders of Israel, thousands of soldiers dressed for battle appeared both in the north and the south. These "angelic soldiers" remained there defending their positions until the "real" Israeli troops and equipment arrived, and then they disappeared. Within twenty days, Israel defeated the Arab forces, and no significant territorial changes occurred. "The angel of the Lord encamps around those who fear him, and he delivers them" (Psalm 34:7).

One of my longtime friends was a major in the Israeli army. He and the soldiers under his command told me numerous stories of angelic intervention that occurred regularly on their maneuvers. We, too, should pray that our own eyes will be opened to the thousands of guardian and warrior angels surrounding us. God still battles for us today.

In the book of Acts, some apostles were imprisoned by the Sadducees, "but during the night an angel of the Lord opened the doors of the jail and brought them out" (Acts 5:19). Herod had already killed John's brother, James. Word was circulating that Herod was persecuting the early Church because he wanted to please the Jewish leaders who opposed Christianity. Later, during the week-long Feast of Unleavened Bread, Herod arrested Peter and threw him into prison, where he was heavily guarded by sixteen soldiers. Herod intended to hold a public trial of Peter after the Passover. Meanwhile, the entire group of believers in Jerusalem prayed for Peter's deliverance (see Acts 12:1–5).

The night before his trial, Peter, bound with chains, was asleep between two soldiers. Suddenly, an angel with a brilliant light appeared and passed through the soldiers, awakening Peter. Instantly, the chains fell from his wrists. The angel told Peter to quickly dress and follow him. They passed unseen by the guards and continued to the entrance gate to the city, which opened in front of them. They walked to the end of the street before the angel suddenly disappeared. Peter said, "Now I know without a doubt that the Lord sent his angel and rescued me from Herod's clutches" (Acts 12:11).

Following his escape, Peter went directly to the house of Mary, the mother of John, where the believers were gathered to pray for his freedom. When Peter knocked at the outer gate, Rhoda, a servant girl, announced to those inside that Peter was at the door. The believers' response was disbelief, and they concluded that the visitor must be Peter's angel.

The human touch in this story is that the Christians were praying for Peter's freedom, but when that prayer was answered and he appeared at the door, they could not believe it. Think about their response, though. Angels were so involved in the daily life of these believers that they considered an angel at the door as a "normal" response to their prayers.

Sadly, such an active belief in the assistance of angels is neither understood nor accepted in many churches today. In losing that belief, we have lost much of our rich inheritance. There was a time when believers not only accepted angelic intervention, but depended on it.

six

Guardian
Angels

For he will command his angels concerning you
to guard you in all your ways;
they will lift you up in their hands.

Psalm 91:11–12

Your guardian angel, personally selected by God for you, is always by your side to shield you from danger, guide you, comfort you and bring God's healing graces to you. Thomas Aquinas believed that each of us has a guardian angel who remains with us forever. No matter how difficult your situation, your loyal angel remains beside you.

The beloved Pope John XXIII was deeply devoted to his guardian angel. He told parents that they should "teach their children that they are never alone, that they have an angel at their side."[1] Another hero of our faith, Joan of Arc, was guided

Making Room for an Angel

Our grandchildren sometimes like me to lie on the bed next to them as they go to sleep. One night my four-year-old grandson was restless and told me, "I don't want to close my eyes because I might see monsters."

I explained that if he asked Jesus to come into his dreams and bring his guardian angel, they would keep the monsters away.

He said the prayer, then he closed his eyes and said, "Grandma, could you move over a little, please? My angel needs more room!"

—Anonymous

by Michael the archangel to become a warrior and take up the cause of France. She held fast to the angel's guidance during her stormy military days and ultimate death. And Saint Jerome was quoted as saying, "How great the dignity of the soul, since each one has from birth an angel commissioned to guard it."[2]

The angel assigned to you is guardian of your body, but also is especially guardian of your soul—that eternal part of you. What a comfort to be aware that these celestial beings are protecting us on our earthly journey. They know the way to heaven—how much lighter and brighter that path has become for us because of their radiant presence.

Guardian angels protect groups of people, as well as individuals. When Moses was leading the Hebrew children out of bondage in Egypt, God sent a mighty angel to guide them to the Promised Land: "See, I am sending an angel ahead of you to guard you along the way and to bring you to the place

I have prepared. Pay attention to him and listen to what he says" (Exodus 23:20–21). At God's command, this angel came to guide His people to a place He had prepared. The angel communicated directly with Moses.

How do we recognize the voice of an angel the way Moses and Joan of Arc did? In some instances, we clearly hear the angel's voice. In other instances, we actually see the angel appear and speak God's will. These angels encourage us to seek God's will and purpose for our lives. Angels communicate in different ways, so it can be difficult distinguishing between your thoughts, an angel's message or the Holy Spirit. And then there is always another possible source, the "angel of light" named Satan. To receive messages from God's angels, we need to improve our listening skills.

The following story involves two of my favorite people in Jacksonville, Florida, Thad McNulty and his younger sister Shannon. As a nine-year-old boy, Thad received a strong interior message that came to him clearly as an urgent, unusual desire to go swimming.

Thad's Desire to "Go Swimming"

I was nine years old when my family visited my grandparents. One morning, I suddenly had the strongest urge to go swimming in their pool. I didn't hear a voice; it was as though someone was telling me that I had to go swimming, and I had to go "Right now!" Normally, this idea would never have occurred to me. It was a rather cool day, and I was a skinny nine-year-old who hated cold water. My brother and two sisters and I also generally played together, so it was odd that I wanted to go for a swim solo.

Nevertheless, I quickly found my mother and asked her permission.

"No," Mom said, "you don't need to go swimming right now."

I insisted that I really wanted to go, which again was a bit unusual since I was the oldest child and always tried to please my parents.

Mom seemed a little irritated, but she relented. "Okay," she said, "but don't be too long."

I vividly remember feeling as if I were on a mission. I just had to get into that swimming pool. I rushed to strip off my clothes and pull on my bathing suit. I ran to the pool and dove in, swimming underwater to the shallow end, where I noticed something to my right on the bottom. It was my three-year-old sister, Shannon! I dove down, pulled her to the surface and immediately started screaming as loudly as I could for my mother.

Everyone rushed out of the house, wondering what all the fuss was about. As soon as my mother reached us, she took charge. She grabbed Shannon, cleared her throat and began administering CPR. By now my siblings, my father and my grandparents were gathered around her. Mom worked furiously to revive Shannon, and initially my sister was unresponsive. My mother was relentless. She continued CPR until she breathed life into Shannon.

The rescue squad arrived a few minutes later. Since Shannon was okay, there was nothing immediate they needed to do for her. Someone had told the next-door neighbor what had happened, however, and the lady had fainted, so the medical team revived her. Then they took Shannon to the hospital, where she spent the night for observation. The doctors guessed that Shannon had been underwater for over a minute, perhaps two, and was very close to dying. All I could think about was how quickly I had responded to the voice telling me to go swimming. Was it the voice of the Holy Spirit or Shannon's guardian angel or mine? I don't know, but I know that I had never sensed anything that urgently before.

—Thad McNulty

In the Catholic Church, the doctrine of guardian angels became official under Pope Clement X, who served as pope from A.D. 1670–76. Before him, Ambrose, Bishop of Milan, who lived from A.D. 339–397, was quoted as saying, "The servants of Christ are protected by invisible, rather than visible, beings. But if these guard you, they do so because of your prayers."[3]

I encourage you to ask the Father daily to send His mighty angels to protect, guide and enlighten you. A beautiful prayer to that effect was written by the Christian monks who composed the Service of Compline (the official evening prayer service in the Catholic Church):

Keep watch, dear Lord, with those who work, or watch or weep this night, and give your angels charge over those who sleep. Tend the sick, Lord Christ; give rest to the weary, bless the dying, soothe the suffering, pity the afflicted, shield the joyous, and all for your love's sake.[4]

Guardian angels, through their constant companionship, help us grow spiritually. They strengthen our intelligence by

An Angel and a Pet

Our entire extended family goes north to a beach during the summer. A family there owns a big dog that has always been great with children. My son, however, has always been terrified of the dog. On this particular trip I prayed with him, asking God to protect him when he and the dog were on the beach together.

Not long after, my son was sitting on the beach while the dog played catch with his owner. The dog would sit beside my son, then run into the water, then come back and sit down, then run into the water, back and forth. This kept up for about an hour. My son came in for a drink of water, so I followed him inside the house. As I held his hand, walking up the beach, I commented, "I am so proud of how brave you were out there, letting the dog sit near you."

My son answered, "The angel sat between me and the dog, so I wasn't afraid."

—Anonymous

speaking directly to our minds, and the end result is that we see our lives through God's eyes. Being in the angels' presence brings the Kingdom of God closer to us. Abiding in God brings angels and the realm of heaven closer. Angels point us to God by encouraging us to raise our souls to the one who is our strength. Their holiness touches our entire being—our minds, our bodies and our emotions. They lift our thoughts by passing on their encouraging messages from our Lord.

Being with a person of deep faith and prayer leads to a similar experience. I have been blessed throughout life to have relationships with many people whom I consider "giants" of the faith, companions along the journey who have lovingly taught me, encouraged me and corrected me. Just being in their presence makes me want to become a better person. Their prayers and love infuse me with goodness, strength and love. The choice to make a pilgrimage to visit holy places or holy people is easily understood in light of the personal benefits we receive. We are really seeking the presence and love of God Himself. The constant companionship of the holy angels helps provide the graces we need for this level of deep devotion to God.

Several guardian angels are assigned to accompany those involved in ministry and provide them with protection, guidance and strength. A few years ago, I was involved in a meeting with a Catholic priest and a lay evangelist who had been graced with the gift of seeing into the spiritual realm. The evangelist frequently saw angels on their assignments. After the meeting, as we were walking to the elevator, he calmly informed me that I had two guardian angels assigned to protect me. I was overwhelmed with gratitude that God allowed two angels to guard me, as I was often involved with counseling dangerous clients released from prison or mental institutions.

I have to confess that in addition to being grateful, I had the fleeting thought that my work must be more important than that of the priest who was with us. (Pride has a way of slipping into our finest moments.)

The evangelist seemed to know my thoughts. He said, "Don't be too proud. Father John has three angels to defend him."

Humbled, I asked God to forgive me, and I thanked Him for His protective care of us both.

Dr. Russ Parker, director of Acorn Healing Trust in England, is a close friend of ours. An author and teacher, Russ once shared the following story about angels guarding him during a difficult time in his life.

§ An Angel Protects a Speaker

A couple of days after my mother passed away, I was scheduled to speak at a conference in London on the subject "Living with Failure." I did not feel like going, but knew that I could not disappoint the people who had registered. My mind was occupied not only with grief, but with my mother's funeral, scheduled to take place two days after the conference.

As I was speaking, I noticed a young man who was disturbed by what I was saying. He would start to approach me during the breaks, but as soon as he would walk toward me, he would change his mind and walk quickly away.

At the end of the day, he seemed to have calmed down. Finally, he spoke with me. "I did not like what you were saying about failures," he said. "I wanted you to tell us how they are stepping-stones to learning, but you did not. I wanted to tell you how upset I was, but each time I approached you, I was stopped by the two men who had come with you."

I told him that I had come alone.

"You must have come with someone," he said. "Every time I came toward you, these two tall men, almost twins, suddenly stepped forward and said, 'Leave him alone; we are protecting him.'"

I didn't see these men myself, but I think he had seen my guardian angels, who knew I was very weak and in pain. I thank God for sending angels to watch me in such times of hardship and need.

—*Rev. Russ Parker*

I also want to let Linda, my assistant at CHM, share a touching story with you. She related the following miraculous incident.

Angels at a Conference

I had been working for Christian Healing Ministries for eight months, and we were in the middle of a leader's conference on healing at a hotel in Jacksonville, Florida. I was still getting used to what it meant to work for this powerful ministry, and I was adjusting to all that my job entailed. Although physically tired, I was nevertheless on a spiritual high from witnessing some amazing things during my recent travels with the MacNutts.

In my short time with CHM, I had seen cataracts disappear from a woman's eyes, a crippled person get out of a wheelchair and walk and a man's withered arm be perfectly restored. In addition to these physical healings, I was seeing God transform people's lives through inner healing and deliverance prayer.

During the weeks that preceded this conference, I had been asking God to "open my eyes." Although I had witnessed amazing miracles, I was impassioned with a desire for more. Judith was the first speaker on the program. As she began her talk, I noticed that she quickly drank her entire glass of water. She was also biting her lip and seemed agitated and nervous, which is completely uncharacteristic of her.

As I was trying to decide what to do to help Judith, something behind her caught my eye. It was like a long flicker of light. I had decided that my tiredness was finally taking its toll, when suddenly there it was again, only larger—and it was moving.

The only way I can explain what I saw is that it looked as though there were an invisible curtain and something was walking out from behind it. Then, in an instant, there were three of them—big, bright and beautiful. They were at least twelve feet tall, and one stood on each side of Judith while the third stayed directly behind her. They didn't have wings, arms, legs or even faces, yet I knew instantly that they were angels. Amazed, I watched as they moved around her, as if ministering to her. Although I could not see their faces, I knew that one of them was looking directly at me. In my mind I heard the angel quite clearly say, "Don't worry. We've got her covered."

Sitting beside me was the chairman of Christian Healing Ministries' board of directors, Lee Ann. She leaned over and asked me, "What do you see?"

I replied, "Angels."

"Well, that makes sense," she said.

I looked at her while trying to keep my composure and said, "What do you mean, that makes sense?"

Just as if this happened every day of the week, she calmly said, "I've been sensing that there is someone in the room who is praying against Judith, so for the Lord to send angels to protect her makes perfect sense."

She was right, it did make perfect sense, but the fact that I was seeing angels did not. I was completely overwhelmed, but I realized that the Lord was answering my prayer. Previously, I had worried that it was a mistake to ask for a glimpse into the spiritual realm, but now I felt nothing but joy. The whole experience lasted about five minutes or so, but they were life-changing minutes.

It has been four years since that day, and I have yet to see any more than small flickers of light, but I often sense the presence of these magnificent, holy angels. I believe God allowed me to see the angels as part of my preparation for working at Christian Healing Ministries. Since that time, Judith and I have been in many challenging situations where I might be tempted to doubt that angels are present. However, having seen them firsthand, I can no longer entertain those doubts.

I believe the Lord also was showing me that it is all right for me to ask for a greater awareness of the reality of the spiritual realm. I was going through a period of self-doubt, and He not only reassured me, but He rewarded me—just what you would expect from a loving Father.

—Linda Strickland

Our Lord loves to encourage and protect us. Since that day when Linda saw the angels standing guard, she has never

An Angel in Blue

A five-year-old boy was on his way to bed for the night. His mother offered to go upstairs with him and tuck him in. "No thanks, Mom," he said. "I'm not afraid. The lady in blue is there for me."

—Anonymous

doubted their presence or their power to protect us against evil. In our world travels, we know that our heavenly guards are alongside us. Thankfully, these heavenly friends are given to us for our entire life journey. Here is one of my personal stories.

Timmy and His Mother

Several years ago, my husband, Francis, and I were leading a healing conference in a large church. The long day had been filled with teaching and lively discussion. We knew that everyone was excitedly anticipating the evening healing service, as many had already told us about their need to receive God's healing touch.

During the service, a young mother came forward for prayer, followed closely by her six-year-old son holding tightly to the folds of her skirt. Tearfully she told us of her deep heartbreak. She was recently divorced from her husband of ten years. The way she carried her body clearly showed her despair and loneliness. Her deepest concern, however, was for her young son, Timmy.

Since the divorce, Timmy had withdrawn more and more from life and had shown symptoms of depression. He missed his daddy terribly and felt somehow that he was to blame for the breakup of the family. A fearful mother's heart had brought her broken son to the Lord for healing.

Unlike most six-year-old boys, Timmy had a face etched with sadness. His eyes were deeply sorrowful. As we laid hands on Timmy and prayed, he began to cry softly. Suddenly, something drew my attention to the ceiling. I looked up, and there, sitting on a wooden rafter high above the cross, was an angel. A brilliant white light surrounded him, and his garment was shining—unlike anything I had ever seen before. His countenance was joyful, yet concerned as he watched us pray for Timmy. I had the distinct impression that he, too, was praying for Timmy.

After the prayer, Timmy tearfully thanked us and returned to the pew with his mother. Occasionally, I glanced at Timmy and noticed that he was looking in the direction where the angel was seated. Excusing myself from the healing line, I slipped into the pew beside Timmy. I asked him if he would mind sharing with me what had captured his attention. By this time he was staring at the angel, his eyes full of wonder.

He hesitated for a moment, and then he slowly said that he saw "a large man sitting on a rafter." He gave me a quizzical look, as if to ask, "Do you believe me?" I smiled and assured him that he was seeing an angel of the Lord.

When I asked Timmy to describe the angel, he gave me an exact description of his hair, clothing, smile and size. I asked him if he was bigger than my husband (who is six foot four), and he said, "Much bigger." I told Timmy he was greatly blessed to see this angel. A broad smile covered his little face. Excitement raced through his voice as he said, "I believe God wants me to know He sent this angel to always take care of me, since my daddy can't be around anymore."

Two close friends who are ordained ministers involved in healing ministry around the world told me these next two stories.

Angels Protect a Minister in the Philippines

During the 1980s I traveled annually to the Philippines to conduct a series of charismatic healing services, usually in Anglican churches. On one occasion, I was asked to hold a healing service on the island of Basilan. You may recognize the name because of the Muslim insurgency there, the reports of forced conversions, abductions of missionaries and even the murder of Christians. Though such events have significantly escalated these days, they had just begun while I was there in 1986.

While I always pray for God's protection and anointing before conducting services, I do not usually pray for angelic protection. But, this one day, I asked God to "ring the perimeter with warrior angels." The service was being held outdoors on the large lawn in front of the small church. People were being dramatically healed, and in their gratitude to God and love for others, they would immediately run back to their barrios to bring others for prayer. A few times during the service, the priest in whose parish I was ministering stopped to tell me that a particular person who had just been healed was Muslim, and now the person was asking Jesus to be Lord and Savior.

About two hours into the service, I noticed a large truck drive up. Several heavily armed soldiers jumped out, quickly scanned the area and fixed their eyes on me. Being an American five feet eleven inches tall, with fair hair and a light complexion, I stood out among the shorter, darker-skinned Filipinos. Dressed as a priest, I was recognized as the leader in a place where Filipino Muslims were being healed and converted by Jesus Christ.

The soldiers had started toward me when, all of a sudden, something spooked them. They were pointing all around the edges of the lawn where the service was being held. They seemed terrified as they quickly made a mad dash back to their truck.

A few days later, I found out what had happened. They were Muslim soldiers coming to kill the person who had led some Muslims to Christ—me! They were advancing and were about to shoot us, when they suddenly saw, circling around the perimeter, a large band of soldiers aiming their weapons at them. Realizing they were vastly outnumbered, the assassins made a hasty retreat.

Thank You, Jesus, for Your warrior angels protecting us that day, and thank You, Jesus, that many people were healed and saved in Your name.

—*Rev. Canon Dr. Mark A. Pearson*

The Archangel Michael Protecting and Celebrating

On my second ministry trip to Belfast, Northern Ireland, I was speaking at St. Anne's church one evening. The previous Saturday, the Shankill Road bombing by the IRA had killed 10 people and left 57 wounded. We weren't sure whether anyone would attend the Monday meeting, but despite the bombing, people came in large numbers.

During the time of worship, I felt the Lord directing me to look upward. There was a huge shining figure, standing with a sword in his hand, at the front and to the left of the nave. I asked God who he was, and He answered, "Michael," which surprised me. When I asked God why Michael was there, He said, "To protect and to celebrate."

I nudged Joseph Sampson, who was standing next to me, and said to him, "Look!"

He looked up and said, "Wow!" Joseph's response confirmed that I wasn't hallucinating. We were truly in the presence of a holy angel.

Later, during the message, I told the story of my angry, unforgiving response to my father's death and how it had adversely affected me for much of my life. When the prayer time came, a large number of people rushed forward to deal with unforgiveness in their own relationships. Many others asked for prayer, wanting to invite Jesus into their lives. At one point during the joyful worship, I looked back over to where Michael had been standing and was delighted to see that he was now dancing.

—Rev. Mike Evans

The following story was written by a longtime friend of mine. It is another example of unseen angelic intervention averting a car accident.

⸱ Angels Prevent an Accident

I was newly elected to our parish council in central Virginia. I had never served on a parish council before, so I was grateful for the chance to attend a summer conference held in Connecticut about Catholic parish life. I went with our dynamic pastor, Father John, and two other wonderful members of our council, Sharon and Larry.

On the road trip, we took turns driving Sharon's spacious car. Arriving in New Jersey, I took my turn driving on the Garden State Parkway. Traffic was moving smoothly, so I was using the car's cruise control. Suddenly we drove into an unusually heavy rainstorm. Within moments, the road began pooling with excess water. On the radio a few days earlier, I had learned about hydroplaning; the advice given was to avoid using your brakes since that could put your car into a spin. However, the only way to get the car out of cruise control was to tap the brakes. I tapped them as lightly as possible. Suddenly the car began to spin.

I knew several cars were in the other three lanes, and I was terrified that our spinning car would hit them. Each spin brought our vehicle closer to the dividing concrete barrier. Totally helpless, I simply called out, "Jesus!"

Praying, we braced ourselves for the inevitable crash. Suddenly, the front fender tapped the median barrier and the car came to a gentle stop. The car was facing forward in the high-speed lane, and all the other surrounding cars were gone. How did this happen? Inspecting the damage, we found a four-inch piece of rubber from the fender hanging down. That was it. The car was fine, and we were fine. We hugged each other in amazement and thanked God for answered prayers.

How were we rescued from what was sure to be a serious accident? Our little group did not see any angels, but there must have been a host of angels protecting us, making rows of speeding cars disappear and guiding our out-of-control car to a gentle stop. We had a great time at our conference and returned safely to our church, strengthened by our experience of radical protection.

—Pat Fitzgibbons

In the following story, when danger approaches in the guise of threatening strangers, a young missionary utters the name of Jesus and is immediately rescued.

An Angel Guards a Missionary

In 1999 I took a year off work for a five-month mission trip to the Ukraine. I quickly found work in a newborn orphan nursery at Hospital #10. With the help of my interpreter, I learned how to get to work on my own, which was rather simple, as the bus stop was directly in front of the hospital. Most days, though, my wait to return home was considerable because the buses were often too crowded to cram in one more body.

It was summertime, so the weather was often sunny and warm. Beside the hospital was a very inviting, paved path down a slope that led into a lovely treed area. One beautiful afternoon, having watched two full buses already go by without stopping, I found myself staring at the lovely path to the park. I knew it was foolish and possibly dangerous to go there alone, but I had twenty minutes until the next bus would arrive. I realized that I could take a short walk and still catch the next bus home.

Walking alone in the lovely cool shade of the trees and enjoying God's creation, I noticed two men walking toward me. I kept walking, not thinking much about them, until they were close enough for me to see their faces. One of the men in particular glared at me with a menacing look. Abruptly, they began to walk straight toward me. I was alone and terrified.

There wasn't really time to pray—the men were only a few meters away—so I said, "Jesus!" Immediately there was a look of utter shock, even disbelief, on both their faces, and they hurried away as if running from something. I don't know if they saw angels, but I will be eternally grateful to the Lord for His protection that day.

—*Jinny Lamont*

Jinny was not permitted to see her guardian angels, but the men's startled reactions indicate that angels appeared to them. What did they see that forced them to run away and leave Jinny unharmed? Mighty, dazzling angels.

A very close friend submitted the following story. She, too, was protected from harm and felt encouraged to know her guardian angel was vigilant in caring for her.

An Angel on an Empty Baseball Field

It was a usual Tuesday morning at home. My daughter, Virginia, and I were in a last-minute search for her library book. I asked her where she had last been reading it.

"Oh, no!" she cried, bursting into tears. "I think I left it at the baseball field."

The night before, we had watched my son's baseball game from the vantage point of the scoring box. It had been too cold to sit in the stands, so we had huddled together. Some of us were watching the game; Virginia was reading.

Few things in my world are more persuasive than my daughter's puppy dog tears, and I was determined to lift her spirits. "I'll take you to school, and then I'll go back and get it," I reassured her. Later, I drove to the baseball field alone. Feeling uneasy as I walked toward the scoring box, I prayed, "Lord, protect me and send Your holy angels to protect me." Whenever I sense fear or hesitation, I utter that prayer almost automatically.

The distance from the parking lot to the scoring box is about the length of two football fields, next to the railroad tracks. As I rounded the corner to the opening of the scoring box (a little metallic shed), I was completely startled as I came upon a man who had obviously spent the night in the structure.

"Oh, hello," I said, trying not to appear anxious. After a very cordial exchange and no book in sight, I headed back toward the car, half trotting, glancing back and hoping the man wasn't following me.

At that moment the Holy Spirit intervened, reminding me how cold the previous night had been, how thin the man's welcome mat blanket was and how hungry he probably was. I bought him breakfast and returned to the baseball field. As I got out of the car, I hesitated. What was I thinking, going back alone into a potentially dangerous situation? I walked back to the shed with another simple yet powerful prayer, "Lord, protect me and send Your holy angels—I really need them now."

When I was fifteen feet away, I called out, "Yoo-hoo," which startled the man. Apparently, he had gone back to sleep after my last visit. "I brought you breakfast," I told him as I shoved the bag into his hands and started backing away.

"Oh, thank you," he said. "Did your friend come back with you?"

"My friend?" I actually turned around, scared that perhaps someone was following behind me.

"Yes, the tall blond guy who was with you the first time," he answered.

Then it hit me: I had prayed—I was protected.

"Yes, he is with me," I answered.

"Thank you so much," he said, "and thank your friend, too."

*"You're welcome," I said and dashed off. This time
I didn't look back. I knew my heavenly Father had
protected me, and even though I didn't see my protector, this lonely homeless man did.*

—*Kathi Smith*

God protected Kathi and allowed a homeless man to "see"
into the spiritual realm. The "tall blond guy" was not threatening to this homeless man—the angel just wanted to communicate that Kathi was not alone. What graces were given
to this poor lonely soul by Kathi's guardian angel?

Our dear friend Father Richard Rohr shared the following
story. He is a Franciscan priest, an international speaker, the
author of many wonderful books on the spiritual life and the
founder of the Center for Action and Contemplation. Father
Richard's moving account of the death of his beloved mother
illustrates how the "veil is thin" during those last liminal days.

A Mother Sees Her Son's Guardian Angel

*As a preface to this story, I would like to say that my
mother was not a pious Catholic. During her life, she
did not tend to talk the way she did in this story, so it
made the moment in question all the more believable
and wondrous.*

*It happened on Thursday afternoon, December 30,
1993. My mother was dying of cancer at the age of
79, and my family and I knew she was nearing the
end. To make the transition easier, we had arranged
wonderful hospice care for her in my brother's home
in Topeka, Kansas. I had come home for Christmas
and was the only one in the house that afternoon. The
others were at work or running errands.*

*My mother had been slipping in and out of conscious-
ness, so I quietly approached the foot of her bed to see
if she was alert. She opened her eyes but did not focus
on me; rather, she focused all of her attention to the left
of me. She was clearly scanning someone up and down,
acting as if there was someone standing next to me.*

I said, "What are you looking at, Mother?"

*With calm, quiet clarity, she said, "Oh, it's your guard-
ian angel." She continued to gaze off to my left side.*

*I looked but saw nothing there, and finally I said,
with some nervousness, "What does he look like?"*

*She looked intently and said, "Well, he looks just
like you."*

*With real disappointment, I said, "Oh, I thought
he would be better-looking."*

*She closed her eyes peacefully, and I never talked to
her again. I myself sensed no presence, but neither did I
doubt her "seeing" this being. She died on the following
Monday morning, January 3, and I was able to celebrate her funeral Mass on the Feast of the Epiphany,
knowing she had left me with one final and wonderful epiphany. All my theological training and years of
ministry had not allowed me to see, fully understand or
even be prepared for what Mother saw—and what so
many see—in those last liminal days and hours when
the "veil is thin" between this world and the next.*

—*Father Richard Rohr*

In order for a father or mother to completely embrace
death, having the assurance that a child—even an adult

child—is cared for is paramount to peacefully "letting go." As Richard's mother approached death, she was allowed to "see" his guardian angel standing beside him, caring for him. With that assurance, she could "go home."

A lovely, older English gentleman whispered this final story about the protective care of our guardian angels to me as we fed birds on a sunny afternoon in St. James Park in London. One of our favorite family outings was to take our young children to feed the ducks and other birds that had taken up residence in the park. One day as we were feeding the birds, this kind man showed up with seeds for the birds, which he happily shared. He started telling me this story. It was one of those indescribable moments where you know God has something He wants you to hear.

A Man Saved from Drowning

The man told me that he had been in the army in World War II and had been stationed in the Mediterranean. On one of his furlough days, he went to the beach with a fellow soldier. He wasn't a strong swimmer, so he knew he should not swim out beyond the shallow waters. He waded out to about his waist, felt safe and stepped out a little deeper, then deeper again. He was having fun.

When he had gone well beyond his usual comfort zone, a sudden rush of current beneath him sucked him under the water. It was a riptide, and it took him out toward open water. He was pulled down very deep, and he couldn't break free from the current. In the grip of this dangerous riptide, he remembered that his grandmother had told him, "If you ever need anything, call on Jesus." At that fearful moment, he cried, "Lord Jesus, help me!"

The instant he prayed, two strong arms wrapped around him and locked him in their grasp. He said that he and his unknown rescuer did not swim to the surface, they shot to the surface. In little more than an instant, his head was above water, and in another instant, he was lying alone on the beach. He sat up and looked in all directions, but no one was around.

After seeing him pulled under the water, his friend had swum out in search of him. The friend later told him, "I saw you struggling and tried to go out and save you, but the current was too strong. I couldn't get to you. How did you get onto the beach?"

In response, the man said, "I'm not sure. Someone in the water pulled me to the surface." He and his friend both went up and down the beach to try to find whoever had saved him, but no one was in sight.

After the kind gentleman told me this story in the park, feeding the birds all the while, he said, "I know my rescuer was an angel."

I have been so privileged to have hundreds of people, both friends and strangers, share their remarkable angelic encounters with me. I hope that as you become more aware of the loving companionship of angels, you will not feel alone on life's journey. Angels love with a limitless love because they are pure love—created by God, who is the source of all love.

In the following chapter, you will read about angels of healing and meet several people whose lives were forever changed by healing miracles involving angels.

seven
___

Angels
and Healing

A few years ago, a man sought my advice concerning an encounter he had with a stranger when he was critically ill in the hospital. He shared his story with detailed precision, as though it had happened the day before. After sharing his story, the man confided in me that this experience had radically changed his relationship with God. He quietly asked, "Do you believe that the doctor was an angel sent by God?"

See what you think as you read about what happened.

An Angel Doctor

A year ago I suffered a sudden heart attack and was placed in Intensive Care, where I was constantly monitored. After numerous consultations, the medical staff

*notified my wife and family that my condition was
severe and that I probably would not live through
the night. I knew that I was dying. I could feel my
life ebbing away.*

*In the middle of the night, as I felt close to death,
an unknown doctor appeared out of nowhere. He
started barking medical orders—not just giving orders—barking orders. "Give him his medication!" As
he was speaking, the nurses were scurrying around
doing exactly what he said. Then without a word, he
disappeared. Within moments, I improved immensely
and rested well throughout the night. By morning I
was totally healed.*

*After my discharge, my wife and I tried without
success to find the doctor who had saved my life. No
one with that name on his white coat had ever worked
at that hospital, and the nurses said they had never
seen him before. There were no orders signed by this
doctor in my medical chart.*

—*Anonymous*

Over the course of my career, I have worked as a psychotherapist in several hospitals. To fully comprehend the
significance of this story concerning a doctor and his treatment of a patient, it must be understood that absolutely no
medicine is administered to a patient without written orders
in the patient's chart by a staff physician. Another significant detail involves the sick man. Most people assume one
must be holy or extremely devout to be visited by an angel.
This man had never given much thought to God, much less

angels or healing. The truth is that God desires healing for His children, and He seldom waits for us to have the faith to ask Him. His love is abundantly given to those in need.

According to the New Testament, healing was and still is central to the message of Jesus, both during His earthly life and today. He never treated healing as a side issue. Unfortunately, over the centuries a lively belief in God's desire to heal has diminished to the point that now, few Christians seek healing from God when they are in need. If they do, they rarely expect anything will happen. Often, this is a case where they have not been taught that healing still takes place today.

The Bible prophesies that in the last days, people will keep an outward appearance of religion "having a form of godliness but denying its power" (2 Timothy 3:5). Yet this power of the Holy Spirit is available to the Church to heal and transform our lives on every level of our being—emotional, spiritual and physical. How is it possible that something so central to the message of Jesus has been lost? As a result, millions of suffering Christians who could have been healed—and nonbelievers, as well—remain sick, and many have died.

Fortunately, many in the Christian faith are being awakened to the wonderful reality that God still heals today. His message has not changed. We have a Savior who "took up our infirmities and carried our sorrows . . . and by his wounds we are healed" (Isaiah 53:4–5). Jesus viewed healing as an essential part of His mission to restore and reclaim God's children from the grip of sin and evil. Healing was His passion. He had a fierce determination to heal the sick, often healing on the Sabbath, which was against the customs of Judaism. Jesus challenged that system every day by extending mercy, forgiveness and healing to those in need.

Ultimately, Jesus shared His mission with His twelve disciples by allowing them to share in His divine power and authority: "He called his twelve disciples to him and gave them authority to drive out evil spirits and to heal every disease and sickness" (Matthew 10:1; see also Luke 9:1). Later, finding that He alone could not adequately help the multitudes of sick—not even with His twelve disciples working alongside Him—Jesus anointed many new disciples.

> After this the Lord appointed seventy-two others and sent them two by two ahead of him to every town and place he was about to go. He told them, "Heal the sick who are there and tell them, 'the kingdom of God is near you.'"
>
> Luke 10:1–2, 9

These others were ordinary people like you and me whom Jesus empowered to spread His Kingdom by preaching the Good News and healing the sick. When the early Church was born after the death and resurrection of Jesus, the Holy Spirit gave this same authority and power to every believer. Numerous accounts of healing are recorded in the Acts of the Apostles. The basic teaching in the book of Acts is that early Christians carried on the mission of Jesus by proclaiming the Kingdom of God, which included doing the work of Jesus.

Today, this same anointing to carry on His work is still available to Jesus' followers. The Holy Spirit equips us with the gifts of the Kingdom, which include "gifts of healing" (1 Corinthians 12:9). To accomplish His purpose of redeeming humanity, God anoints believers, along with His holy angels, as instruments of healing. Mother Teresa of Calcutta said of herself that she "was a pencil in the hand of God."[1]

Angels Bring Healing

I haven't thought of angels too much in my lifetime, but recently when I called upon them for help to relieve pain in my knee, I felt their immediate presence in the room. I experienced total relief. Amazing!

—Anonymous

All healing is from God. He is the source; we are simply His hands.

In his excellent book *The Healing Reawakening: Reclaiming Our Lost Inheritance* (Chosen Books, 2006), my husband, Francis, provides a scriptural, historical and practical guide to the essential ministry of healing. He addresses the mystery of the decline and resurgence of the healing ministry—how the Church lost its healing ministry over time and then regained it in this century. Now more than ever, we need to see the fullness of the healing message of Jesus restored as part of our rich inheritance.

Angels of healing are on assignment and carry "healing in their wings" from God's great heart of compassion to those who are suffering. These angels contain within their being the life (power) necessary to grant healing on every level of our humanity. As they draw near someone receiving their ministry, the entire environment alters. Where fear or pain existed, a deep sense of peace fills the person's heart and mind, and he or she often experiences a euphoric feeling of well-being, accompanied by warmth and a brilliant light. Emotional or physical pain either diminishes or disappears completely. Recipients of these angelic visitations express feelings of intense well-being followed by an experience of great love, as in the following story.

§ Angel Healing Temporomandibular Joint Disorder (TMJ)

When I was a young mother, I was baking while my daughter played contentedly in her walker. She squealed with delight, blowing bubbles and laughing the way only children can, every time I sang a hymn or talked to her. As I worked, I tried to dismiss the excruciating pain that spread from my jaw through my ear and down my neck. I was all too familiar with this pain. It had been chronic and worsening over the past year. I had been diagnosed with TMJ, and our doctor had referred me to a specialist. Pain medication was not an option because I was breast-feeding my daughter. The specialist was also out of the question, as my husband and I were trying to live on one income and 90 percent of it went to pay our mortgage. I stood in the kitchen and prayed, "Lord, I am in so much pain and we can't afford the help I need. It hurts so badly, but I'm not going to worry about it anymore. I turn this over to you."

That night I crawled into bed, my jaw still raw with pain. I began praying for others who I knew needed help. I felt such incredible love for others—I think it had something to do with my worship in the kitchen earlier that day.

Suddenly, I felt a hand on my face. For a second I thought my husband had placed his hand there, but I quickly dismissed the thought. His hand wasn't large

*enough to span my wide cheekbones. I could feel a
right thumb on my right jaw, and then fingers taper-
ing from my temple to the jawline on the left side of
my face. There was a deep, penetrating heat emitting
from the fingertips.*

*I lay there awestruck, surrounded by a presence of
immense love. The pain was lifting and, for the first
time in over a year, I felt relief. I knew I was being
healed. All I could say was, "Thank You, Jesus."*

*With deep gratitude I wept, and then I fell into a
deep, restful sleep. When I awoke the pain was completely gone, and I have been pain-free for all these
years. I'm not sure if it was the hand of an angel or the
Lord, but this experience taught me that Jesus sends
help when we turn our pain over to Him.*

—Anonymous

The following story relates the angelic encounter of a
young mother after she and her child were involved in an
automobile accident on a snowy road.

An Angel Bandages an Injured Mom

*It had been snowing off and on all day, and as the
temperature dropped, the roads began to form dangerous "black ice." Driving the short distance to the
babysitter's was worrisome enough, but I dreaded the
thought of the half-hour drive back home.*

*After picking up my daughter and buckling her into
the car seat, I felt a bit calmer. A few minutes into our
drive, she was fast asleep, her breathing relaxed and*

peaceful. Traffic crept along slowly because drivers were cautious on the icy roads. At any given moment, a car could slide out of control. Thankfully, I was almost home after a relatively peaceful ride. Over the bridge, and we would be safe.

When I stopped at the last light before the bridge, I took my truck out of four-wheel drive. When the light turned green, I started slowly across the bridge, but then I sped up when I saw that other cars weren't having any problems.

In an instant, it felt as if the road had disappeared out from under me. I tried to steer, but found that I had completely lost control. Sliding across three lanes, I hit the cement divider. Rebounding in the other direction, I careened across the same three lanes and smashed into the cement siding along the bridge's edge before finally coming to a stop.

Shaken and confused, I realized that the traffic was coming toward me. I was facing the flow of traffic, and there was a lot of blood around me. My baby was screaming. I began to panic, unable to determine the source of blood.

As I was unzipping my daughter's snowsuit to look her over, I felt a tap on my shoulder. I turned around, and there stood a huge man. He calmly said, "Your baby is just fine. You are the one who is bleeding."

He opened a briefcase, and inside were different-shaped bandages. The man reached through the window, tilted my head back and gently put the bandage on a gash on my chin. I was in awe of his gentleness and the kindness he showed. In the distance I could hear sirens. The ambulance slid on ice as it approached my truck.

As the paramedics checked us, I heard the driver call someone on the radio and say, "Get the city to sand this dangerous bridge—now!"

Confused, the paramedics asked me who had bandaged my chin. When I turned to point out the tall man, I couldn't find him. After looking everywhere, I realized he was nowhere to be found. I had not seen him pull up in a car, nor had I seen him leave. It was really kind of eerie.

After going to the hospital for twenty stitches on my chin, it was nice to be home. I felt grateful that my daughter was sleeping soundly in the next room, without a single scratch on her body. I called my mother to tell her that I had been in an accident. When I told her about the mystery man, she chuckled and said, "You were lucky your guardian angel was looking after you."

—Anonymous

When angels appear in human form to accomplish an assignment, they often assume a nonthreatening appearance to avoid frightening people. This young mother was agitated and concerned about her daughter, so the kind man with the briefcase immediately brought her comfort. He told her the baby was fine and proceeded to help her, then he was gone.

After completing their mission, angels who assume physical form will frequently disappear in an instant, without a trace. They never desire to be the focus of our attention or gratitude. They quietly carry out God's will before returning to their invisible spiritual bodies. They possess the ability to override the laws of nature when they alter their appearance or perform miracles with the power of God.

Here's another story about an angel helping a mother and child.

A Scruffy-Looking "Gardener"

In the fall of 1974, our son Matthew was seven months old and curious about everything. He spent his time crawling around our ground-floor apartment and exploring his little world. One day while watching him from across the room, I saw him pick up a leaf that had fallen to the floor from a houseplant. He put it right into his mouth. I ran to him, but by the time I reached him, he had swallowed it. I tried retrieving the leaf with my finger, but could not.

The next thing I knew, my little son was staring at me with frightened eyes, unable to breathe. The area around his mouth turned bluish—cyanotic—which I later learned was a sign of oxygen loss. Panicking, I hoisted him into my arms and ran outside, crying for help.

"My baby can't breathe! Help! My baby can't breathe!" I shouted.

Right outside the entryway was a scruffy-looking gardener trimming bushes. I had never seen anyone like him working in our apartment complex before, and I never saw him again. He immediately took my baby in his arms and pressed a grimy finger into Matthew's mouth. He fished around for a few moments before pulling out the leaf in one whole piece.

Tearfully, I thanked the man profusely. All these years later, I have no doubt that the scruffy gardener was actually an angel sent to save my son's life. I give all the thanks to God for His loving care and for His holy angels.

—Dorothy Welsh

Instead of the usual tall, bright angel, this one appeared as a scruffy gardener. Outward appearances do not seem to concern angels when they are performing an urgent rescue. Tragedy usually strikes swiftly, with little warning, often when no one is available to help. At times such as these, angels materialize and lend their assistance before mysteriously disappearing.

The next story challenges us to pray without ceasing when a beloved family member is in desperate need of God's healing.

A Grandson's Healing

A child was slated to have surgery for a tumor on his clavicle. He was only fourteen years old, and the doctors' prognosis pointed to a sarcoma. To the horror of the entire family, the outlook was grim. The morning of the surgery, his grandmother was sitting one hundred miles away, at her home. She was feeling discouraged about the boy's chances for survival but kept up her prayers for her beloved grandson.

In the middle of her prayers, someone knocked on the front door. Somewhat irritated by the intrusion, she opened the door to find a man dressed in a white suit standing there. He asked if he could have a few minutes of her time. Usually a very gracious woman, her short response was, "I can't talk to you. I'm far too worried about my grandson's surgery."

Unperturbed and with a smile, the man in white said, "Don't worry, ma'am. I'm positive your grandson is going to be fine."

As she closed the door, she became upset by this intrusion into an already difficult morning. She immediately opened the door to tell the man so. To her surprise, she found no trace of him. Only a matter of seconds had passed. He had disappeared. She began to feel that there was something unusual about this visitor. More than the rarity of seeing a man dressed in a white suit in the chill of winter, something in his demeanor was strangely pacifying. He seemed to know her situation. Returning to her prayer spot, she felt a deep sense of reassurance about her grandson's condition.

Several hours later, the phone rang. It was her daughter reporting that her grandson was doing fine, but that something unusual had happened. After a final analysis of the clavicle bone, where the tumor had registered on the tomogram, the doctors were surprised to find that the tissue was completely normal. The tumor had disappeared. Thankfully, no surgery was necessary. She rejoiced with her daughter, thanking God for her grandson's healing and for the angelic visitor wearing a white suit.

—Anonymous

One can only imagine the chilling fear that enveloped this entire family with a diagnosis of a sarcoma, a cancerous tumor, in their child. This kind of tumor usually requires extensive treatment involving surgery, radiation and chemotherapy. The prognosis was grim even with medical intervention. Two miracles surround this story. The first was that in the midst of this grandmother's fear and distress, a messenger angel in a white suit brought hope and comfort by telling her that her beloved grandson would be fine. The second was that God sent angels to bring His healing power to this little boy.

Here's another story from a grandmother.

An Angel Appears to Bring Comfort and Healing

When our grandson was severely injured in a ski accident, I immediately took a flight to be with him. After arriving at the hospital and talking with my son and his wife, I realized that my grandson's condition was much worse than expected. Relieving his exhausted mom and dad one evening, I stayed beside him all night, holding his hand and watching him as he lay in a deep coma, not moving or stirring in any way. Being so close to the situation, I had difficulty praying, but I took comfort in knowing that many dear friends were covering us in prayer.

That night, looking at my grandson's small, motionless body, I sat there with tears streaming down my cheeks—they would not stop. The door opened very quietly and a large, beautiful, dark-haired nurse came in the room. She quietly and lovingly said to me in an accented voice, "Dry your tears, lady. Do you think that because your baby is sleeping, God is sleeping?

God doesn't sleep. He does His best work when our children are sleeping. He's healing that child right now, so quit your crying."

I closed my eyes and rubbed them dry, but when I opened them again, she was gone. I immediately went to the nurse's station and asked to see her so I could thank her. A blonde nurse behind the desk with several others told me that no nurse fitting that description had been on duty that night.

Now, tell me that was not an angel sent to comfort me in my distress, far from home as I was watching my precious little fellow fighting for his life. Through the intervention of an angel and the prayers of many people, my beloved grandson experienced a complete recovery over the course of time.

—Anonymous

This beautiful angel brought encouragement to a grandmother's heart that her beloved grandson would be healed. The angel's gentle reminder that God is not sleeping brought peace, hope and comfort to the entire family.

A friend of many years who is ordained told me the following marvelous story about a member of her congregation and his experience after a dangerous surgical procedure.

A Cradling Angel

Meeting for prayer before surgery, a congregant confessed his apprehension to his minister, so they prayed together for God's healing. Following the prayer, she told him, "Remember that the angels are with you."

Thankfully, the man's surgery was a complete suc-cess. That same evening, when he woke up from the sedation, underneath him, cradling him like a baby, was a large angel. The angel rocked and cradled him all night in the hospital bed and disappeared when the sun rose.

The man reported that tremendous strength and love flowed into him from the angel. He excitedly reported to his minister, "The angel was beautiful beyond description. I'll never be afraid of anything ever again."

—*Anonymous*

At O'Hare International Airport in Chicago, I went into a shop to buy a magazine. Susan, the cashier, had an angel pin on her lapel, so I asked her if she believed in angels. "Oh yes," she said, and proceeded to tell me about her encounter with a healing angel who came when she was close to death. I noticed that as Susan shared her story, not one person came into the gift shop in that extremely busy airport. Our meeting seems to have been a divine appointment.

Susan's Angel

Susan had been suffering on and off from undiagnosed severe abdominal cramping for some time. Eventually she was rushed to the ER, where she underwent an extensive medical workup. She was admitted to the hospital, and her doctor arrived and gave her the test results. Her condition was very serious. Her entire body had been affected by toxins.

Around midnight, suffering alone in her room, she cried out to God for relief. In spite of the medication, her body was enveloped with pain and her abdomen was alarmingly distended. She felt as though she were dying. A patient hospitalized for terminal cancer heard Susan's cries and came to her bedside. She gently placed her hand on Susan's forehead, asking, "What's the matter, Sweetie?"

Susan couldn't help but notice how terribly thin and frail the woman looked. The woman wore a blue scarf that covered her thin hair, cute bunny slippers and the ever-present hospital gown.

Susan tearfully answered, "I'm in such terrible pain, and the doctors can't help me. I don't mind dying, but the pain is unbearable—I feel so alone."

The visitor smiled kindly and said, "Would you like me to pray with you?" Susan nodded. The visitor took out a vial of oil and said, "Do you mind if I anoint you for healing?" Susan nodded again, and the visitor anointed her while praying quietly for what seemed like a long time.

During the prayer Susan's abdomen, formerly distended, returned to normal size, and the pain slowly decreased. Susan was overjoyed and kept thanking her visitor. Finally pain-free, she fell into a deep, peaceful sleep.

In the morning, the doctor was surprised to see Susan sitting up in bed. He later told her he had not been sure she would live through the night. After thoroughly examining her, he said that he could not find anything wrong with her. She was totally healed.

> *Susan proceeded to tell the doctor about her night visitor, at which point he looked very confused. He said, "Please describe your visitor." After Susan gave him a detailed description, including the bunny slippers, the doctor replied, "That's impossible. The woman you are describing died at 8:00 P.M. last night."*

Evidently, in order to minister God's healing graces to Susan, this healing angel assumed the physical form of a patient who had recently died. Such stories as these surpass our understanding, but remind us that we have a merciful heavenly Father who hears the cries of His children.

The following story serves as a powerful reminder that angels function in many ways to answer in times of great need. We also catch a glimpse into heaven from a child who has been there.

An Angel Takes a Drowning Boy to Heaven

Like most mothers, my worst fear has always been that something bad could happen to one of my children. Last year, that fear became a reality. It was a typical summer evening spent watching our oldest son's Little League baseball game. After the game, the team and their families got together for a pool party and cookout. Our four-year-old son sat a few feet away from us on his towel, eating a hot dog with the "big boys." Halfway through my meal, I realized he was no longer on his towel. Many of the younger children had finished eating and were happily playing. Suddenly I had an overwhelming urge to find my son.

I immediately went to the pool, but didn't see him. I scanned the area in and around the water, looking for his little red swimsuit, but I didn't look carefully at the deep end. Unable to find him, I had my husband join my search.

We called for him for about seven minutes, and then we heard screams. There on the concrete lay my precious son, who had been pulled out of the deep end of the pool. He looked lifeless, bloated and blue. My husband immediately started CPR.

This cannot be happening, I thought. Not to my child.

Kneeling behind my son were two of our friends who were praying. Falling to my knees, I prayed as well that the Lord would please give me back my son.

I found out later that my son did not have a heartbeat for the first five minutes of CPR. After twelve minutes, the ambulance arrived. At that point, he was breathing again and had a heart rate of 120 beats per minute. Arriving at the hospital, he was quickly intubated. His lungs were swelling, and he was having seizures and posturing, which is a sign of brain damage. The doctors wanted him transferred to the children's hospital. Things weren't looking good for our little boy.

When we arrived at the children's hospital, the ICU doctor informed us that our son was in critical condition, but that there was a chance for survival. He also said to anticipate a five-day waiting period during which our son's brain could begin swelling.

After the doctor left, we asked God for complete healing. When we were able to see our little son, he had tubes down his throat and into his lungs, one arterial line into his heart, numerous IVs and a bladder catheter. He was a pitiful sight, but he was alive. I felt impressed then to read Psalm 18, which says, "He reached down from on high and took hold of me; he drew me out of deep waters. He rescued me" (verses 16–17).

After our son was extubated on Tuesday, he first asked to see his brothers and then asked for a hamburger. Exactly one week after his horrible accident, he was released from the hospital. A child who was expected to die—or at least to suffer severe brain damage—was being taken home on his granddad's shoulders.

A few days later, I asked my son what he could remember from the accident. He told me, "An angel came and picked me up, and we flew through walls, clouds and through you, Mommy." He told me the angel had long white clothes and that they flew to heaven, where there was a door with jewels all around it. "When they opened the door," he said, "it was snowing in there."

I was very careful not to put words into his mouth. The only time I asked him for more details was when I asked if he had seen his uncle in heaven. He said he had seen him and that he looked "just like Jesus—all his boo-boos were gone." He told me that Jesus had held him and that there were lots of angels everywhere.

As he was describing this to me, I asked him if he was ever afraid, and he said, "No, I was with Jesus." I asked if he would like to go back to heaven again, and he said, "Yes, but Jesus is coming here."

This experience has given our entire family a boldness to shout from the mountaintop what the Lord did for our son, and we praise Him for His sovereignty.

—*Anonymous*

Jesus' restoration of this precious child to his family brought indescribable joy. This child leaves us with a powerful prophetic word from his time in heaven—"Jesus is coming here." These words are filled with great hope for every believer. Not only are heaven and the angels real—Jesus is coming.

eight

Unholy
Fallen Angels

> And having disarmed the powers and authorities, he [Jesus] made a public spectacle of them, triumphing over them by the cross.
>
> Colossians 2:15

Both good angels and evil angels, or demons, occupy the unseen spiritual realm. For a more comprehensive understanding of this, I have included this chapter on fallen angels. At a time when movies, television, novels and music glorify and sensationalize evil and distort the facts, we need to educate ourselves about the spiritual battle we face. The following accounts tell of my own experience with evil, which began at the age of seven in my childhood home.

By all outward appearances, the hideous creature looking up through the heating grate was not of this world. Even now, many years later, I have difficulty describing the sheer evil I felt as its dark eyes pierced my soul. I was frozen with fear and unable to scream, run or even look away, like those nightmares where no sound emerges when you scream and you are unable to move. We were locked together in that place, and time stood still.

In my heart, I knew it had come for me. This creature had materialized in order to "capture" me. I was only seven years old, but somehow I knew this. My father was a stone's throw away preparing dinner. If only I could call out for help. As grotesque as the creature was, I felt drawn to the force of its presence, like a moth to the flame. I was terrified. Then "it" uttered a sound, a raspy, guttural whisper—definitely not human, more animal sounding—and at once its spell was broken. Suddenly my feet moved, my breathing returned (I cannot remember breathing) and I was on full alert. I stumbled backward, screaming like someone riding on a roller coaster. My father heard my cry and caught me in an instant, grabbing me by my shoulders and demanding to know why I was screaming. My mind swirling, I began babbling about a frightening creature in the basement that wanted me and how I had seen it in the grate. Fortunately, I was not a child given to lying or exaggerating. To my great relief, Dad believed me.

Since the only entrance to the basement was through a door just outside our home, Dad quickly rushed to unlock the basement door, which was secured by a large padlock. He threw open the door, switching on the light as he walked into the damp, musty space. I followed him from behind, but not too closely. Consciously, I was struck by my father's courage. He did not hesitate or try to talk me out of what I had seen. That was not the first or the last time I saw Dad's bravery. He continued to search for the creature. We both realized that, whatever it was, it could not have escaped. Had it become invisible to our eyes?

My father tried to help me untangle my thoughts. "Exactly what did you see?" he asked.

Worried that he might not accept my description, I tried to shrug the incident off as unimportant, not worth his time. He kept insisting that I focus and describe it. Oddly enough, I sensed that he believed me and would not laugh at me. In my best effort, I gave him a detailed description of the creature.

His first response was very interesting. He asked, "How did it make you feel?" I had the distinct impression that he had experienced this "being" himself at some earlier time.

We soon returned to the safety and warmth of our living room, where my mother joined us. After we told her what had happened, she asked the same question. My parents seemed concerned about the impact the experience had on me. Surrounded by their loving presence, I felt safe enough to explore my feelings. Releasing the paralyzing fear that was beginning to fade away, I explored the possibilities. The "thing" I saw in front of me was as real as my flesh-and-blood parents, yet was not a flesh-and-blood being like us. Instead, it was a dark evil spirit appearing from another realm or dimension. Even now, I am so grateful that my parents understood the reality of that spiritual dimension well enough to help me.

This evil "thing" was my first experience of seeing into the invisible realm. It would not be my last. My unnerving experience that day faded into the background of my very happy childhood. The honest and direct way my parents dealt with my experience allowed me to release any fear attached to the experience, but still I wondered. I continued to embrace life as it unfolded before me, a life filled with a loving family, many wonderful friends and a growing faith nurtured by a small church of committed and loving people.

As a child, I was enveloped in a community of faith made up of strong women and men of God who readily accepted His goodness and love for them. They gladly shared all that they had, materially and spiritually, with everyone. My early childhood models of what it meant to be a Christian were solid and scripturally based, for the most part. The reality of the unseen world was readily incorporated into my church's faith journey, but was not completely understood. Superstitious ideas were mingled with truth, and this ultimately led to confusion. For instance, ghosts were freely accepted alongside Satan and his demons. Sorting through these unseen negative forces was discouraged, with the lame explanation that if you focused too much attention on these beings, they would "notice you" and somehow would create havoc in your life. Pastors and Sunday school teachers quietly redirected my questions or observations on the topic of dark spirits to the love and goodness of God.

Was it a question of perception? Or too much abstract thought? Why was everyone so guarded about evil, the mysterious force that seemed to defy understanding? All I wanted to know was whether or not these spiritual beings, the embodiment of evil, existed. And if they did, how could I develop a clear, balanced understanding about them? Realizing my probing questions were unacceptable to church leaders, I did what most people do—I disengaged from the topic of evil in order to be accepted. Then I had another encounter.

Ten years had passed; now I was a teenager. Anything concerning the spirit realm had receded into the lower realms of my awareness. Now I was obsessed with dating, cheerleading, my appearance and my friends. My mind was open to God, and occasionally that "small voice" inside would grasp my attention and tug at my heart, but overall, my social life had taken over.

But then one Saturday, I had another encounter with evil in my childhood home. Feeling sick, I was hoping I only had a 24-hour bug. I had an exciting first date that evening with the captain of the basketball team, a young man I had admired at a distance. I was desperate to recover quickly, so I was alone resting in my brother's spacious room, watching TV, when I became aware of a presence watching me from the open doorway. I could not see its face, but I felt its presence.

"It" appeared to be well over six feet tall and exuded a negative, terrifying energy that quickly snapped my brain to full alert. I remember thinking that it was attempting to communicate something urgent to me. Then it suddenly moved toward me. Terrified, I released a piercing scream that stopped its approach. When I screamed again, it moved quickly to the door and disappeared into the adjoining room—my bedroom.

My father (who had had ten years to recover from the last encounter) and my older brother, J. C., ran into the room, wild-eyed with concern. I told them a "man" was in the house and was now in my bedroom. My father quickly entered my room through one door, while my brother entered at the same moment through the only other entrance. They searched the room and closet and found no one. Again, my father gently questioned me not only about what I had seen, but about how it affected me. I realized that this encounter with what

I now call the "shadow man" was additional evidence of the vast spiritual realm that surrounds us.

Why was I given these exposures to the unseen realm? After serious reflection, I realized that God had allowed me to see these negative, disturbing images. God wanted me (and wants all of us) to be aware of this invisible realm of the spirit where angels and demons exist. I made a personal decision that day to learn as much as possible about this serious subject so I could help people.

I have shared these experiences so that you can begin to understand the importance of this unseen realm. Jesus Christ gave us the basic information we need concerning demons or fallen angels. When Jesus walked on this earth, He battled Satan on a regular basis. Unfortunately, in this scientific era we have become disconnected from the knowledge of evil because the subject cannot be analytically proven. Our understanding and acceptance must come with simple, childlike faith in the Savior who died and rose again, who conquered sin and evil, and who defeated Satan, the prince of this world.

Who Is Satan?

"The reason the Son of God appeared was to destroy the devil's work" (1 John 3:8). God created Satan, a mighty cherub (see Ezekiel 28:14), along with the entire angelic realm whose original purpose was to love and serve Him in loving obedience. God had given the angels a free will, and at some point Satan and his demons chose to rebel against the Lord. The Catholic Church's Fourth Lateran Council (A.D. 1215) described it this way: the "devil and the other demons were indeed created naturally good by God, but they became evil by their own doing."[1] Several Scriptures mention the battle in heaven that took place between the holy angels and Lucifer (Satan)—for example, Revelation 12:7–9:

> Michael [the archangel] and his angels fought against the dragon, and the dragon and his angels fought back. But he was not strong enough, and they lost their place in heaven. The great dragon was hurled down—that ancient serpent called the devil, or Satan, who leads the whole world astray. He was hurled to the earth, and his angels with him.

This account of Satan's fall from heaven with a third of the angelic realm reveals that a large number of demons serve Satan (see Revelation 12:4).

The third-century theologian Origen refers to Ezekiel 28 as a graphic description of Satan's magnificence and beauty, followed by his disobedience and rebellion. Ezekiel is writing about the king of Tyre, but these descriptions are also seen as referring to Satan himself:

> You were the model of perfection,
>> full of wisdom and perfect in beauty . . .
> every precious stone adorned you:
>> ruby, topaz and emerald,
>> chrysolite, onyx and jasper,
>> sapphire, turquoise and beryl.
> Your settings and mountings were made of gold;
>> on the day you were created they were prepared.
>> You were anointed as a guardian cherub,
>> for so I ordained you.
> You were on the holy mount of God;
>> you walked among the fiery stones.
>> You were blameless in your ways

from the day you were created
till wickedness was found in you. . . .
So I drove you in disgrace from the mount of God,
and I expelled you, O guardian cherub. . . .
Your heart became proud
on account of your beauty,
and you corrupted your wisdom
because of your splendor.
So I threw you to the earth . . .
you have come to a horrible end
and will be no more.

Ezekiel 28:12–19

Ezekiel's details of this king's downfall could not apply to a mere human, especially the great splendor of the king's countenance and the reference to being "anointed as a guardian cherub." The "holy mount of God" is the throne room of God where the cherubim dwell. No matter how the fall occurred, Satan's rebellion resulted in his loss of status as a noble prince in the heavenly court.

When Jesus' 72 disciples returned from their missionary journeys to spread the good news of the Kingdom, they reported with delight to Jesus that "even the demons submit to us in your name" (Luke 10:17). Jesus, filled with joy, replied, "I saw Satan fall like lightning from heaven" (verse 18). The disciples' successful deliverance experiences reminded Jesus of the original fall of Satan and his demons from heaven.

We catch another glimpse of Satan's fall in the writings of Isaiah:

How you have fallen from heaven,
O morning star, son of the dawn!

You have been cast down to the earth,
    you who once laid low the nations!
You said in your heart,
    "I will ascend to heaven;
I will raise my throne
    above the stars of God;
I will sit enthroned on the mount of assembly,
    on the utmost heights of the sacred mountain.
I will ascend above the tops of the clouds;
    I will make myself like the Most High."

Isaiah 14:12–14

Most Bible scholars believe that Isaiah was describing the rebellion of Satan in these verses. The name "morning star" in Hebrew is translated as "Lucifer" in the Latin Vulgate translation. Lucifer (or "light bearer") is one of the many names commonly used for Satan.

In his wonderful book *Angels*, Billy Graham said,

> Lucifer was not satisfied with being subordinated to his creator. He wanted to usurp God's throne. He wanted to be worshiped, not to worship. Satan's desire to replace God as ruler of the universe may have been rooted in a basic sin that leads to the sin of pride.[2]

Pride is considered the worst of the seven deadly sins that all of humanity share. Satan personally committed this sin of pride, and today he continues successfully enslaving humans in this area of weakness. Most of our competition for power, possessions and prestige (the three *P*'s) is rooted in pride.

Satan in the New Testament

Satan's adversarial activities are scattered throughout the Old Testament, but in the New Testament his activity increases. The obvious battle between Jesus and Satan looms large at the very beginning of the synoptic gospels of Matthew, Mark and Luke. After Jesus is baptized by John the Baptist in the Jordan River at the onset of His ministry, the Holy Spirit leads Jesus into the wilderness, where He fasts and prays for forty days. As Mark reports, Jesus was "being tempted by Satan. He was with the wild animals, and angels attended him" (Mark 1:13). Matthew and Luke expand the story of this encounter with lengthier accounts of the three temptations Satan employed. Jesus was in a weakened state of hunger following His forty-day fast. Satan visited Him, thinking He would be vulnerable to temptation—especially in the offer of bread. Clearly, Satan did not fully understand the person of Jesus. Mighty angels were surrounding Jesus to offer Him their strength and protection.

As we explore the exchange that took place between Jesus and Satan, notice that Jesus quotes Scripture in response to each temptation. Also, the reverse is true; Satan quotes Scripture to Jesus. It is fascinating to observe that in the gospels, Jesus typically does not quote Scripture and usually speaks with His own authority—except in the case of this trial with Satan.

In the first temptation,

> The tempter came to him and said, "If you are the Son of God, tell these stones to become bread." Jesus answered, "It is written: Man does not live on bread alone, but on every word that comes from the mouth of God."
>
> Matthew 4:3–4

In the second temptation, the devil took Jesus to Jerusalem and had Him stand on the highest point of the Temple.

If you are the Son of God, throw yourself down. For it is written: "He will command his angels concerning you, and they will lift you up in their hands, so that you will not strike your foot against a stone."

verse 6

Jesus answered Satan with another Scripture: "Do not put the Lord your God to the test" (verse 7). This second temptation gives us insight into Satan's knowledge of not only Scripture, but of the angels' mission to guard Jesus. Without a doubt, Satan could see numerous angels standing protectively around Jesus, waiting for the command to battle this fallen cherub who was now their enemy. But Jesus waits. This is the first appearance of Satan in the gospel accounts, but this is not his first meeting with the angels, nor with Jesus. The first time was in the heavenlies, when God created the angels and they dwelled in loving unity with Him. Now Satan's relationship has changed from one of unity and love to one of hostility and conflict. Satan was using everything in his arsenal to divert Jesus from His earthly mission of reclaiming God's world.

The third and final temptation revealed the devil's ultimate desire for Jesus to abandon God the Father and worship Satan himself. This was Satan's only hope of diverting Jesus from His final destination, the cross, which ultimately would reclaim this world and God's children.

The devil led him up to a high place and showed him in an instant all the kingdoms of the world. And he said to him, "I will give you all their authority and splendor, for it has been given to me, and I can give it to anyone I want to. So if you worship me, it will all be yours."

Jesus answered, "It is written: Worship the Lord your God and serve him only."

Luke 4:5–8

It is important to understand that Satan rules over the kingdoms of this world, and Jesus did not dispute it. But having conquered each of the temptations Satan brought, Jesus commanded, "Away from me, Satan!" (Matthew 4:10). Luke reveals Satan's determination to continue tempting Jesus throughout His life: "When the devil had finished all this tempting, he left him until an opportune time" (Luke 4:13). According to the gospel accounts, Satan attacked Jesus again and again, but Jesus never yielded. Our Lord showed tremendous tenacity, not to mention authority, whenever He encountered Satan or his demons.

Jesus has given this same authority to His Church, His followers, to conquer the powers of evil. In addition to our own authority against the enemy, we have the aid of God's angels, who are committed to helping us overcome the devil. Pope John Paul II taught Catholics that "the battle against the Devil [Satan], which is the principal task of St. Michael the

Not Guardian Angels

During a change in schools, our son began to suffer from anxiety again. While talking to him about the changes, he said, "I see these horrible things on kids, and they're not angels. They look really scary, and it hurts me. Some of the kids have them, and I hardly ever see angels at this school."

—Anonymous

Archangel, is still being fought today, because the devil is still alive and active in the world."³ (This same pope is reported to have taken part in two deliverance episodes.)

The major theme in the New Testament is this continuous battle between the Kingdom of God, established by Jesus, and the kingdom of Satan. We engage in the struggle between these two opposing kingdoms every time we pray for the sick, pray against evil or witness the redeeming power of the Holy Spirit pushing back darkness and ushering in God's light. All Christians are engaged in this conflict, whether they are aware of it or not.

Sadly, many believers are ill-equipped to deal with the onslaught of the enemy and his demons. The great British author C. S. Lewis cast light on this when he wrote, "There are two equal and opposite errors into which we can fall in relation to the devils. One is to disbelieve their existence. The other is to believe and to feel an excessive and unhealthy interest in them."⁴ Lewis emphasized the importance of understanding that Satan, the created, fallen angel, is not equal to God, the Creator of the universe.

Peter proclaimed Jesus' mission when he talked about

> how God anointed Jesus of Nazareth with the Holy Spirit and power, and how he went around doing good and healing all who were under the power of the devil, because God was with him.
>
> Acts 10:38

The name *Jesus*, which the archangel Gabriel gave to Mary for her child, means "God saves." Even Jesus' name indicates His mission. He saves mankind from Satan, sin, sickness and ultimately death.

Fallen Angels/Demons

We must realize that Jesus' teachings about evil were not mere words. Hearing Jesus' words, people responded by saying that His teaching was new. Look at this instance when Jesus and His disciples went to Capernaum:

> When the Sabbath came, Jesus went into the synagogue and began to teach. The people were amazed at his teaching, because he taught them as one who had authority, not as the teachers of the law. Just then a man in their synagogue who was possessed by an evil spirit cried out, "What do you want with us, Jesus of Nazareth? Have you come to destroy us? I know who you are—the Holy One of God!"
>
> "Be quiet!" said Jesus sternly. "Come out of him!" The evil spirit shook the man violently and came out of him with a shriek.
>
> Mark 1:21–26

Try to imagine the startled reactions in the small, crowded synagogue that day when Jesus was teaching about the Kingdom of God. Recognizing Jesus, a demon screams out with fear and indignation. Perhaps those gathered were already wondering about this Jesus who was teaching with great authority. Then, without warning, one of the congregation (perhaps a neighbor) falls to the floor, screaming and thrashing around. In an altered, tormented voice, the demon speaks to Jesus in agony, imploring Him, "Have you come to destroy us?" (Note that the plural "us" is used.) Before Jesus can respond, the demon reveals the marvelous truth recognized by demons, if not by man—"You are the Holy One of God"—which points out Christ's divine origin.

Without hesitating, Jesus sternly and with authority says, "Be quiet!"—which literally means "Be muzzled!" Then Jesus commands, "Come out of him!" Two commands, spoken with superior authority and power, released that poor soul from years of torment and suffering. The onlookers responded amongst themselves, "What is this? A new teaching—and with authority! He even gives orders to evil spirits and they obey him" (Mark 1:27).

Mark's gospel, the shortest of the four, makes thirteen references to Satan or to casting out demons. As in the previous account, the demons always reacted fearfully when Jesus was present. He did not always directly confront the demons, but they were flushed out of the darkness when He appeared.

Demon is the English word used to name these powerful, malevolent fallen angels. It is derived from the Greek word *daimon*. The exact number of fallen angels is unknown, but Scripture refers to at least a third of the angels being cast out of heaven. Some are awaiting judgment in chains, and some wander the earth and torment mankind. "God did not spare angels when they sinned, but sent them to hell, putting them into gloomy dungeons to be held for judgment" (2 Peter 2:4). *Hades* is the term the Greeks used to designate the place where the demons were sent to await judgment. It is a mystery why some demons are in chains while others are allowed freedom until the final judgment. Jude also refers to these fallen angels: "And the angels who did not keep their positions of authority but abandoned their own home—these he has kept in darkness, bound with everlasting chains for judgment on the great Day" (Jude 1:6).

The Organization of Demons

Just as the holy angels are organized in an angelic hierarchy with those most powerful at the top, so the demons are also ranked according to their power. Paul warns us of the might of this unseen world:

> Finally, be strong in the Lord and in his mighty power. Put on the full armor of God so that you can take your stand against the devil's schemes. For our struggle is not against flesh and blood, but against the rulers, against the authorities, against the powers of this dark world and against the spiritual forces of evil in the heavenly realms.
>
> Ephesians 6:10–12

In his *Inferno*, Dante organizes the demons into nine circles of hell, basing the circles or levels on the seven capital sins. He leaves the final, deepest level for Lucifer. In the tradition of Church writings, these levels are not clearly defined, resulting in ambiguity. However, in our ministry experience confronting the demonic, we find that some demons are much more powerful than others and that they are organized in some kind of hierarchy of power.

Jesus refers to this hierarchy when He encourages His disciples to persevere in dealing with demons. A father had brought his mute son, who was possessed by an evil spirit, to Jesus' disciples and had asked them for help. The father explained his son's condition to Jesus, saying,

> Whenever it seizes him, it throws him to the ground. He foams at the mouth, gnashes his teeth and becomes rigid. I asked your disciples to drive out the spirit, but they could not.
>
> Mark 9:18

This is one instance where Jesus expressed His impatience and anger at the unbelief in His disciples. He tells the father to bring his son to Him. "When the spirit saw Jesus, it immediately threw the boy into a convulsion. He fell to the ground and rolled around, foaming at the mouth" (verse 20). Jesus rebuked the evil spirit, which then shrieked, convulsed the boy and finally left him. Jesus lifted the boy up by the hand and returned him, completely freed, to his overjoyed father.

When Jesus and His disciples were away from the crowd, the disciples began to question Jesus about why they could not cast out that particular demon. In the past, they had prayed successfully for other afflicted people to be liberated. Jesus replied, "This kind can come out only by prayer" (verse 29). This insight seems to suggest that not only are there different kinds of demons, but there are certainly differing levels of power among them. Through experience and through watching others who have deliverance ministries, we have seen that the most common types of demons are easily categorized into three major groups: *occult spirits, spirits of sin* and *spirits of trauma*. Francis's book *Deliverance from Evil Spirits: A Practical Manual* (Chosen, 2009) explains these categories in more detail, but let's briefly look at them here.

Occult Spirits/Demons

Just as demons display varying levels of power, they have names that indicate their position of authority or their mission. As we know, the highest-ranking demon is Lucifer or Satan, a fallen cherub. Those directly under him have proper names: Antichrist, Beelzebub, Pasuzo (mentioned in Assyrian and Babylonian mythology), Leviathan, Asmodeus (referred to as the king of demons in ancient Hebrew writings), the

Destroyer and Azazel (known in Jewish mythology as a demonic figure). The apocryphal book of Tobit mentions an instance in which the holy archangel Raphael defeats the demon Asmodeus, who is tormenting Sarah by killing her bridegrooms on their wedding nights. God assigns Raphael to intervene and rescue Sarah and her new bridegroom, Tobiah. After the demon is cast out following prayer, Raphael then pursues Asmodeus to Egypt, where he binds him to prevent his return.

Occult spirits have odd-sounding names that usually indicate their level of power and authority in the spiritual realm. The "open door" that allows these spirits into a victim's life correlates to a person's direct involvement in occult activity. Scripture gives many warnings about the dangers of getting involved in occult activities. Unfortunately, occult spirits exist in many forms and hide behind seemingly innocent fronts. Protecting oneself and one's family is essential. Sources or practices such as Wicca, black magic, voodoo, consulting Ouija boards, tarot cards, fortune-telling and witchcraft carry a darkness that is all too often hidden until the spirits have caused serious consequences to an individual. Our churches need to teach about the dangers of these occult practices in order to avoid the devastation that follows.

Spirits of Sin

Names signifying a human vice or sin characterize this second large category of demons. These demons are assigned to tempt people to enter into sinful behavior and draw victims away from God's love. They are identified by the names of sin they try to lead us into, such as Murder, Lust, Hatred, Addiction and Envy.

Satan and his demons are creative and clever with their temptations. Remember the dialogue between Eve and the serpent in the Garden of Eden? The serpent questioned Eve about whether she had heard God correctly, thereby sowing doubt in her mind (see Genesis 3). Scripture refers to Satan as the "father of lies" (John 8:44). No truth is found in him. Demons in this second level manipulate a person through lies to entice him or her into making sinful choices. Then the door is open for a spirit of sin to continue its evil actions. Before long, the individual who continues to make sinful choices becomes "a slave to sin" (Romans 7:14). The sin, which first was a choice made in a moment of weakness, moves from being a temptation into being a sinful act, and then into becoming a sinful habit that ultimately turns into a stronghold of the enemy.

Freedom from sin comes to us through the steps of personal repentance, renouncing sinful behavior and accepting the merciful forgiveness of our Lord Jesus.

> When you were dead in your sins . . . God made you alive with Christ. He forgave us all our sins, having canceled the written code, with its regulations, that was against us and that stood opposed to us; he took it away, nailing it to the cross. And having disarmed the powers and authorities, he made a public spectacle of them, triumphing over them by the cross.
>
> Colossians 2:13–15

Forgiveness is always available as a grace, a gift to us because of Jesus' sacrifice on the cross. Through His death, He atoned for all sin once and for all. Isaiah prophetically wrote that the Messiah would be the final sacrifice for the sins of all mankind:

> He was pierced for our transgressions, he was crushed for our iniquities; the punishment that brought us peace was upon him, and by his wounds we are healed.
>
> Isaiah 53:5

By its very nature sin wounds our spirits, leaving us not only in bondage but in need of deep healing. Once we have repented and received God's forgiveness, it is also often necessary to pray for inner healing concerning the wounds of sin. The power of the cross brings salvation, forgiveness and healing. While praying with many wonderful broken children of God, I have found that those who do not "feel" forgiven are often the ones who have not prayed for healing of the wounds of sin that may remain even after the sin has been forgiven.

Jesus disarmed every enemy of our souls when He chose to die on Calvary's cross and make a public spectacle of them. He flushes the demons out of their hiding places in the darkened recesses of people's hearts and forces them into the light, thereby triumphing over them. In ancient times and sometimes in today's world, when a commander and his army conquer the enemy, he parades the shamed soldiers and their weapons through the main public places, thus making a public spectacle of them to show who is triumphant and who is totally defeated. When we are facing our enemy, we have to remember that he has already been defeated by our Lord Jesus. We also have to apply our Lord's healing power to our struggles with our fallen human nature so that we can experience freedom from sin and all of its effects.

The following story reveals the major role the holy angels play in dealing with evil.

§ Praying for an Ex–Gang Member

A youth director called on me to pray for a teenage boy who came from a violent background of gangs and drugs. The boy was beginning to attend church. I was to meet him, along with a team of prayer ministers and his pastor, in the church basement. As I walked down the steps toward the basement, I heard a voice yell out my name very loudly, saying, "We know about you and who you are, and you can take your invisible friends and sentries with you because we are not going anywhere."

The verse "The God of peace will soon crush Satan under your feet" filled my thoughts (Romans 16:20), and as I spoke it out, calm and peace seemed to wash over us all. The teenage boy became quiet. As we approached this young man, however, he began to squirm as if he were uncomfortable. He complained out loud that "they" needed to let him go and stop holding him down.

I thought he was addressing whatever was afflicting and oppressing him. When asked who was holding him down, he responded that the "guards" we had brought with us were restraining him. After returning home, I felt impressed to look up the dictionary definition of sentry. *Encarta Dictionary defines a sentry as "somebody who is assigned to keep watch and to warn of danger, especially a member of the armed services who guards entrances and exits."*

—Robin Morrison

Spirits of Trauma

Spirits or demons of trauma seem to be the most common category of evil spirits that afflict people. These demons have names like Rejection, Fear, Grief, Hatred, Rage and other names that represent our emotional wounds. They are assigned to intensify and distort the existing emotion in us that is the result of unhealed emotional trauma. Some of these traumas begin in early childhood, when a child is vulnerable and immature. For example, an intense fear or anger can be present within a person's memory, making the person vulnerable to demonic attacks. In his book *Deliverance from Evil Spirits: A Practical Manual*, my husband comments,

> We have found that even before birth a baby can recognize if he or she is wanted; and if he is not, a spirit of rejection can hook in. From then on, the person will be prone to rejection, which may be intensified by the spirit of rejection. We can compare this to stepping on a rusty nail (the natural wound), which is then invaded by a tetanus infection. The spirit (demon) intensifies the rejection and tries to block anything that might heal it, like affirmation or love received later on in life. People affected by these spirits may or may not feel that a spirit is present; but they will definitely sense that they are not free in these areas and that their fear or anxiety (or whatever other emotion is agitated) is beyond their ability to control.[5]

The marvelous good news is that we have a Savior who brings His healing love to these emotional wounds, thereby freeing us from demonic attachments. Prayer for emotional wholeness is commonly referred to as "inner healing" or "emotional healing." Inner healing prayer, guided by the Holy

Spirit, reaches into our deepest emotional pain, releasing us from emotional bondage, as well as from possible demonic interference. The following story shows how angels help in this healing process.

Inner Healing Angel

During an intense time of personal inner healing, I was curled up in a fetal position on the floor, in great pain, as the Holy Spirit was ministering freedom and healing. I had my eyes closed and could feel a cool breeze. I asked the person ministering to me if he could please close his sliding patio doors. He said they were closed. I could still feel the breeze and could even see the curtains to the windows and patio doors swaying gently.

I asked him to turn off the air conditioning since the "breeze" was a bit cool. He said it was not on but that he could feel the breeze also, and turned to see the curtains moving. I felt strongly impressed by the Holy Spirit that it was the movement of angels' wings. Soon, I began to see translucent outlines of them—like light shadows and outlines brighter than the room. As I watched, I could see that one of them was pouring something over my friend who was praying for me, and I asked him if he was having the sensation of "liquid" flowing over him. He looked at me, shocked, and asked how I knew this since it was precisely what he was experiencing.

This visitation and "divine gentle breeze" lasted for the rest of the prayer time. When my friend would walk "through" a space that an angelic being was occupying, he would feel an amazing presence even though he couldn't see it.

—*Robin Morrison*

Inner healing touches us in our areas of deepest human suffering, those of the heart, mind and spirit. When past experiences have deeply wounded us, we carry the memories of these experiences and the emotions associated with them. In contrast to the strengthening and life-giving effects of positive memories, painful memories can distort our emotions, leaving a crippling effect in our lives. All too often people live as prisoners trapped in the bondage of their deep wounds.

Isaiah speaks of the words and mission of Jesus when he writes,

> The Spirit of the Sovereign Lord is on me, because the Lord has anointed me to preach good news to the poor. He has sent me to bind up the brokenhearted, to proclaim freedom for the captives and release from darkness for the prisoners.
>
> Isaiah 61:1

Jesus, with His life-transforming love and power to heal, safely delves into our fractured hearts to heal our brokenness and set us free.

A simple definition of inner healing is when Jesus, who is the same "yesterday, today, and forever" (Hebrews 13:8, NKJV), takes the memories of our past and heals us from those emotional wounds that still remain and affect our daily lives. With His love, He can fill all those places in us that have long been left empty. He can drain out the poison of past hurts and resentments. We can ask Jesus to go back to the time when

Angelic Memories

During a time of deep inner healing, one of the memories that
the Lord brought back to me was of my "very happy family"
members playing with me and protecting me in my room when
I was a toddler. Curious, I asked my mom about how I used to
play as a toddler, and she reported that I was always talking and
laughing with my "imaginary" friends, telling her their names
and what they were doing or how they were dressed.

—Anonymous

the emotional injury occurred and free us from the effects of
that devastating wound that still remain in the present. This
process involves two things: bringing to light the things that
have hurt us, and then praying to the Lord to free us from the
binding effects of those hurtful events. Jesus' love transforms
people by healing their crippling emotional wounds, allowing
them to then discover their true self that He created.

Paul instructed us to "be transformed by the renewing of
your mind" (Romans 12:2). God's truth also breaks the lies
that we have believed about ourselves, which often result from
the harsh judgments others make about us. I am always astonished to hear the numerous lies that a beautiful child of God
carries within his or her brokenness. People tend to believe lies
involving their value, lies that create a distorted self-image,
but also lies that greatly distort their image of a loving God
and Savior. Word judgments that are spoken against us like
"you are stupid" or "it's too bad you aren't pretty like your
sister" are some of the lies people commonly hear and believe. God's own love fills, restores and heals people, though.

"And hope does not disappoint us, because God has poured out his love into our hearts by the Holy Spirit, whom he has given us" (Romans 5:5).

A few years ago, I was walking down a street in Scotland with two friends after a healing conference had ended. We walked past a woman sitting on a blanket on the sidewalk. Just as we came up to her, she starting screaming at us, "Get away from me! Stop! Don't get close! Don't hurt me! Help!"

Her volume was so loud that we attracted the stares of a number of bystanders. We were so uncomfortable with the barrage of words coming from her mouth that we hurried our pace to get past her. Visibly shaken, one of my friends asked what that was all about. I told her I believed there was a demonic entity within this woman, and she was reacting to God's presence.

According to Billy Graham,

> Demonic activity and Satan worship are on the increase in all parts of the world. The devil is alive and more at work now than at any other time. The Bible says that since he realizes that his time is short (Revelation 12:12) his activity will increase. Through his demonic influences, Satan does succeed in turning many away from true faith; but we can still say that his evil activities are countered by the holy ones of the angelic order. They are vigorous in delivering the heirs of salvation from the strategies of evil and cannot fail.[6]

These thoughts from one of the world's foremost spiritual leaders help us understand the daily battle in which we are engaged. Many Christians choose simply to avoid all thoughts about this dark realm because they do not like to think about unpleasant subjects. Jesus never forgot that

He had an enemy, and He remained aware of the enemy's influence.

The good news is that Jesus has given us His authority and power to protect ourselves and those we love. Everyone can learn how to pray for protection from demonic interference and incorporate these prayers into daily life. When Jesus' disciples asked Him to teach them to pray, He responded with the Lord's Prayer. The second half of it says, "Lead us not into temptation, but deliver us from the evil one" (Matthew 6:13). I believe our Lord was instructing us to pray for protection against the evil one, Satan himself, a personal entity who desires to harm God's children, not some vague cosmic evil with little power.

As we prepare for the day, saying a prayer of protection each morning can become as natural as getting dressed and brushing our teeth. Most of us learned the Lord's Prayer by memory, including "deliver us from evil." The more accurate translation is "deliver us from the evil one," a much less abstract statement. This prayer calls God's angels into a protective stance. If you carve out time to bless your spouse, your children and your friends, then cover each one with God's protection (including praying for the assistance of God's holy angels), how different your day will be. Your outer garments protect you from the natural elements, but God's spiritual covering protects you from the assaults of the enemy. Realize, too, that we should pray not just for our personal friends, but for our wider social communities, including the government.

Over the many years of our shared ministry, Francis and I have interviewed thousands of Christians concerning their prayer lives. Sadly, what we discovered is a tragic loss that should be a major concern of our leaders. Christians who

ANGELS ARE FOR REAL

come to church every Sunday have never learned to pray
with each other in their homes. When we ask the simple
question at our conferences, "How many of you can remember your father ever praying with you in his own words when
you were sick as a child?" the response is about 3 percent.
When the same question is asked about mothers praying, it
rises to about 20 percent. This statistic represents a tragic
reality. If you are a pastor or a teacher, you can test this
by asking people this question yourself. In his book *The
Prayer That Heals: Praying for Healing in the Family* (a
wonderful book for anyone seeking a deeper prayer life),
my husband noted,

> This percentage is remarkably consistent in all parts of the
> United States; the hands raised are seldom over 5% (for fathers). The only exception was among the students at Oral
> Roberts University where about 50% could remember their
> fathers praying with them. On the other hand, at one retreat
> for 100 seminarians not a single one could remember his
> father praying with him. It is small wonder, then, that after
> ordination they may have difficulty feeling comfortable with
> spontaneous prayer. I have asked the same question in various
> other countries with much the same result. At one gathering
> of 2000 people in Korea, only one hand went up.[7]

The reason for this neglect has to be that parents did not really
think anything would happen when they prayed. Consider
for a moment what message is given to a child growing up
in a Christian home where loving parents do not embrace a
life of prayer together. What is modeled? As adults, children
adopt about 80 percent of their parents' values. If Mom and
Dad do not value prayer, and if they seldom communicate

—◦ 188 ◦—

it as a need, chances are their children will feel inadequate and awkward when trying to pray spontaneously later in life.

Couples in Christian marriages rarely pray together, either. Perhaps the lack of emphasis on prayer when they were children has limited their ability to pray out loud in their own words. When I was working as a marriage counselor earlier in my career, I stumbled onto this reality with my clients. Couples who had focused on doing everything in their power to guard their relationship from the negative forces in our culture still ignored a shared prayer life. Eventually, their marriages started crumbling under the strain of daily life. Many of these marriage partners were sent to me for counseling by one particular judge before she would consider granting them a divorce. The very first recommendation I gave was to begin praying together every morning before going to work. This usually resulted in a startled response, along with various objections. After offering couples some suggestions and books on prayer, I sent them home with an assignment to start praying together. Before long, they recognized a remarkable transformation in their attitudes through prayer, not to mention receiving the additional graces they needed in order to love and forgive each other. Suddenly their intimacy increased, and they started to see each other through the eyes of Jesus.

We have been entrusted with the remarkable capability of loving with God's own love and lifting one another up daily into the light of His healing presence. We also can concentrate our prayers on protecting and defending those we love from evil. How do you begin this life-changing journey of praying with loved ones? Start now in simple ways. Praying together at home is such a beautiful experience and is so easy to learn. Together you can turn your hearts to God. He will meet you in that time of prayer. Remember, His longing for you is always greater than your longing for Him. He loves you and will be completely attentive to your needs and desires.

Your Authority in Christ

God has empowered Christians to take authority against evil in the name of Jesus. He has advised us to shield ourselves with His protection. It is vitally important to do as Paul tells us in Ephesians:

> Put on the full armor of God so that you can take your stand against the devil's schemes. . . . Stand firm then, with the belt of truth buckled around your waist, with the breastplate of righteousness in place, and with your feet fitted with the readiness that comes from the gospel of peace. In addition to all this, take up the shield of faith, with which you can extinguish all the flaming arrows of the evil one. Take the helmet of salvation and the sword of the Spirit, which is the word of God. And pray in the Spirit on all occasions with all kinds of prayers and requests. With this in mind, be alert and always keep on praying for all the saints.
>
> Ephesians 6:11, 14–18

When our children were young, we visited a Christian bookstore and found them a complete toy set of Roman armor detailed with this Scripture from Ephesians. When we gave the armor to them, we explained the meaning of the Scripture in simple ways that they could understand. Our son was six years old at the time, the perfect age for practicing how to engage in a courageous battle against dark forces.

After all, he already had several Nintendo games that empha-sized the importance of fighting dark forces and winning. He walked around our home for hours fully dressed for battle, cutting his sword through the air at imaginary opponents. I recall vivid images of him as he tried to eat dinner with the helmet firmly in place. For a few nights, he actually wore the armor to bed so he would be ready for battle at a moment's notice. I would quietly enter his room after he was sound asleep and remove the armor. I took care to place the sword securely at his side, just in case he needed it.

Without a doubt, you are protected by God's invisible angelic army. However, the main message in Ephesians 6 is that you must protect yourself by praying to the One who has already defeated our enemy. Paul instructs us to "stand" our ground, be strong and ask God to release the army of heaven to defend us. The following story relates a time when the army of heaven did just that for someone.

The Army of Heaven at Our Side

I asked the Lord if my guardian angel was the one who had protected me from an especially severe spiritual attack while I was in seminary. The answer was yes. On that occasion, I was sitting in our chapel before the service. I used to go early to spend some quiet time with the Lord, so my pew was empty except for me. My eyes were closed, but after a while, I felt an enormous evil force coming at me from the opposite end of the pew. I looked over and saw this woman whom I had been avoiding because I had sensed an evil presence about her. She apparently had moved to my pew from the back of the church, where she had been sitting when I arrived.

*Overwhelmed by the evil emanating from her, I
asked the Lord to protect me. At once, I felt a huge
holy presence between the woman and me, and the
evil force felt as though it was completely blocked
off. The woman exited quickly, leaving me to my
prayers.*

*Later I was told by someone with the gift of discernment that the woman was a witch who had been
sent to the seminary to bring spiritual harm to the
students. Eventually she was expelled. My guardian
angel protected me from evil at the Lord's command.*

—Rev. Hazel L. Wilkinson

This story reminds me of the prayer in Psalm 35:

> Contend, O LORD, with those who contend with
>   me;
> fight against those who fight against me.
> Take up shield and buckler;
> arise and come to my aid.
> Brandish spear and javelin
> against those who pursue me.
> Say to my soul,
>   "I am your salvation." . . .
> May they be like chaff before the wind,
> with the angel of the LORD driving them away;
> may their path be dark and slippery,
> with the angel of the LORD pursuing them.
>
> Verses 1–3, 5–6

Forming your own personalized prayers to meet each situation is best. Over time and with more experience in embracing an intimate relationship with the Holy Spirit, prayers will flow freely from a place of childlike trust and faith.

> In the same way, the Spirit helps us in our weakness. We do not know what we ought to pray for, but the Spirit himself intercedes for us with groans that words cannot express. And he who searches our hearts knows the mind of the Spirit, because the Spirit intercedes for the saints in accordance with God's will.
>
> Romans 8:26–27

Sometimes the deepest cry of the human heart during trials and intense suffering cannot be expressed in words. The Holy Spirit hears our silent cry and conveys our needs to the Father's compassionate care and protection.

We certainly do not want to focus too much attention on spiritual warfare in an anxious, worried way, but we need to pray daily for protection. In spiritual battle, we can assume that Satan will not ignore any personal weakness that can serve as an avenue to break through our defenses. Just as Jesus was tempted by Satan on several occasions, we, too, will be confronted with every tool in Satan's arsenal that might cause us to stumble and fall. Satan either will tempt us in areas of vulnerability, or he will assign demonic forces to oppress us, creating emotional apathy or depression. These assignments can produce negative thoughts, confusion, extreme agitation, anger, dullness, fear or paranoia, resentments, discouragement or grief. We realize all of these conditions can have natural, emotional sources, but interference from the demonic can make them worse and increase their severity. Physical problems can also be rooted in demonic assignments against us, producing problems such as sleeplessness, lethargy, headaches and nausea.

When Jesus called Satan the father of lies, He was alerting us to guard against allowing the enemy to discourage or confuse us. Jesus freed those who had fallen under the influence of demons, and He continues today to surround us with His mighty angels. To the apostle Peter, Jesus said, "Satan has asked to sift you as wheat. But I have prayed for you, Simon, that your faith may not fail" (Luke 22:31–32). In His eternal love for us, Jesus continually intercedes on our behalf to our Father. "Because he himself suffered when he was tempted, he is able to help those who are being tempted" (Hebrews 2:18). Over the years, we have prayed for thousands of people suffering from spiritual oppression, and we have rejoiced in the healings we have been privileged to witness.

The Holy Spirit gives us the power, through the authority of Jesus, to command our demonic enemies to depart and leave us in peace. This prayer of command is different from the prayer of protection we say each morning, which is more a prayer of petition addressed to God. But a powerful prayer of command confronts the enemy forces that are focusing their assaults against us or our loved ones. The church father Origen wrote, "Christians have nothing to fear, even if demons should not be well disposed to them; for Christians are protected by the supreme God . . . who sets his divine angels to watch over those who are worthy of such guardianship, so that they can suffer nothing from demons."[8]

Once you become a Christian, you have the spiritual authority to pray for protection from the demonic realm. "Submit yourselves, then, to God. Resist the devil, and he will flee from you" (James 4:7). Powerful commands of release can be short and simple. Jesus simply commanded, "Leave him," or "Depart from her," or "Satan be gone," or "Come out"—short, but incredibly effective.

What I have presented here is found in traditional Christian teaching, but we cannot fully understand it unless we come to grips with certain realities:

1. Evil is something we cannot overcome by simple human goodwill and teaching. Evil is, at its root, demonic. It is too powerful for us to overcome through our own abilities.

2. Jesus came for the purpose of overcoming evil (see 1 John 3:8).

3. Evil cannot be overcome solely through teaching ethical values. Overcoming evil requires the power of God, which is given to us by the Holy Spirit.

4. "Through prayer for healing and deliverance, we become channels for Jesus to heal and to free people (as well as institutions and society) from the evil that weighs them down."[9]

5. The good news is this: "I want you to be wise about what is good, and innocent about what is evil. The God of peace will soon crush Satan under your feet. The grace of our Lord Jesus be with you" (Romans 16:19–20).

Here is a prayer of command and petition as an example to get you started:

Lord Jesus, please send Your holy angels to help me (and my family or . . .), to guide me, to protect me from sickness and accidents and from any evil spirits who are trying to harm or influence me.

I command any spirits who are not of Jesus Christ to depart and leave me [or . . .] and go to Jesus Christ [to be dealt with].

Lord, cleanse me of my sins [specifically repent if necessary] and fill me with Your Holy Spirit. Fill my mind with Your light, fill my will with Your strength, fill my body and emotions with Your health. Fill my entire being with Your life and Your love. Let me love You, God, with all my being, with my will and with my mind. Let me share Your vision for my life and fill me with Your love for people, especially [name those you care for]. Let me see reality and the world as You see it, and let me love people by sharing in Your love for them. Let me become like You, Jesus, so that as Your Word says, "I live now not with my own life but with the life of Christ who lives in me" (Galatians 2:20, JB).

In addition to your own prayers, remember that you are not alone in the battle. Jesus Himself is praying for you: "My prayer is not that you take them out of the world but that you protect them from the evil one" (John 17:15). The angels of God, especially Michael and the mighty warrior angels under his command, also are constantly engaged in this ongoing battle with Satan and the demons. They battle with you and for you. "The angel of the LORD encamps around those who fear him, and he delivers them" (Psalm 34:7). The angels shield you from harm because of God's great love for you.

The Veil
Is Thin

*H*opefully after reading this book about true-life stories of angelic intervention, you have come to realize that angels are real—not only real, but actively involved in your life and in the restoration of the Kingdom of God. As God opens your eyes and heart to the dynamic spiritual realm that surrounds you, you may behold visions, angels and other aspects of God's majestic realm. Remember Linda's story in the chapter on guardian angels? She prayed for God to open her eyes to "see" into the spiritual realm, and God allowed her to see three angels standing guard around me as I was teaching. Linda later said that it was obvious to her that the angels had been there all along in a different dimension.

God may graciously allow you to see, feel and experience His Kingdom when you are in need. Jesus said to His disciples, "I tell you the truth, you shall see heaven open, and the angels of God ascending and descending on the Son of Man" (John 1:51). What a great source of encouragement it becomes to know that God has created the mighty angels as loyal companions and friends who guard you on your journey.

I would like to conclude this book with the story of a time in my life when the "veil became thin" between earth and heaven, a time when I released two "mothers" into God's loving care. During my happy childhood growing up in the small town of Jackson (population 1,120) in eastern Kentucky, I was blessed to have two remarkable and deeply spiritual women who lovingly shaped my emerging self.

Elsie, my biological mother, met the love of her life, my father, Joe Sewell, when she was engaged to another young man. She said from the moment she saw Joe standing on the street corner in that sleepy little mountain town, she knew in her heart that he was meant to be her husband. My dad responded to his first sight of her with extraordinary boldness, following her car until it came to a stop. He then walked up to the car window and announced, "I don't know who you are, but we're going to marry."

Shortly after that day, they were happily married. They spent 33 years together, until she was called home to heaven at the young age of 61. As a child, I frequently witnessed my parents' displays of affection. Though their relationship was not perfect, I never doubted their deep love for one another. I also have a wonderful brother, J. C., who is fourteen months older than I am. The two of us always felt wrapped in the cocoon of our parents' love, as well as the love of our next-door neighbors, Lizzie and Alex Strong. The Strongs had moved next door to my mother when Mom was a young girl. Because Lizzie was a teenager when she married Alex, she and my mom (who was only a few years younger than Lizzie) became lifetime best friends. Dad and Alex, who were as close as brothers, started a business together.

Lizzie had always dreamed of having a large family, but sadly found that she was unable to conceive. After a period of grieving their tremendous loss, Lizzie and Alex gathered my brother and me into their empty, hungry arms, where we joyfully remained until they, too, were called home.

Growing up this way was so magical. Anytime my parents were too busy, distracted or tired to deal with my growing needs, I would slip next door, where I knew I would be embraced with love, warm cookies and milk. My childhood was fashioned by a loving God into a unique, nurturing environment where I was happily content to explore my world with wonder and trust. Also included in that world were many other surrogate parents—Sunday school teachers, Girl Scout leaders, teachers and parents of my dear friends. The circle of love grew daily in that friendly little town, allowing my true self to emerge in that net of safety. I received such an outpouring of love from so many sources that I truly believed the world was a good place, never realizing things were about to change.

Without warning, a major crisis intruded into that happy world. One day soon after my mother's sixty-first birthday, she suffered a massive cerebral hemorrhage. One moment Mom was healthy, the next moment she was fighting for her life. She was rushed to the hospital in Lexington, a hundred miles away from Jackson, and was immediately placed in ICU. I was working in a psychiatric unit in a Boston hospital when I received the urgent call. I immediately caught a plane home to be by her side.

Our faithful friend and country doctor, Robert Cornett, came from Jackson to the hospital and went into emergency surgery with Mom. Hours later, he emerged from surgery to find us in the waiting room. We could tell by his face that the news was grim. The prognosis was devastating. "She probably won't survive more than a few days due to massive bleeding in her brain," he told us. "If she does survive, her brain will have only minimal function."

We were crushed by his words. Hours blended into days as I sat by her hospital bed and prayed for a miracle. I kept encouraging Dad, saying that she would recover, but it soon became apparent that Mom was slipping away. I was young and unprepared to deal with losing my beloved mother. She was everything to me, a constant source of love and care, wisdom, counsel and joy. She taught me about the God whom she loved and served, about Jesus, her Savior and healer, and about the power of the Holy Spirit. She instilled in me a deep love of Scripture.

In my mind's eye, I can still see Mom in that cozy favorite chair in our home, reading her Bible and praying. People always stopped by for prayer or wise counsel. Many were healed of various illnesses or restored in their spirits by praying with Mom. Her deep, personal faith in God's goodness and love for us has had a profound impact on my life.

The day Mom died, I intensely believed I could not live without her. Up until that moment, I had been pleading with God to heal her. As I stood silently praying beside her bed, an ICU nurse commented to me that she could not understand what was keeping my mother alive. She continued by saying, "Every major system in her body is shutting down."

When I turned back to search Mom's face, I realized that she was desperately holding on until we released her. But how could I release someone who was everything to me? During that agonizing moment, I did what she had taught me to do—I turned to Jesus. I asked Him to give me the grace and the courage to release her. I felt as though time stood still. A strong presence surrounded us—Mom in that hospital bed and me beside her, a fearful child. I felt physically supported by strong arms, and a great peace enveloped me. My fear was ebbing away in the light of that presence.

As I gazed at Mom, I watched the strained tension melt from her beautiful face and a dazzling light literally glow from within her. Her pain was gone, and she was ready to go to Him, the lover of her soul. She had passionately loved Him in this life, so she longed to go to Him now. I could hear the words of the Song of Solomon, which she had read to me many times: "My lover spoke and said to me, 'Arise my darling, my beautiful one, and come with me. See! The winter is past . . .'" (Song of Solomon 2:10–11).

Crying softly, I heard myself saying to her, "Don't worry, Mom, it's all right; it's time for you to go with Jesus. We'll be fine." Those words were the ones her spirit had been waiting to hear. She had always been the ultimate caretaker. Now she knew we were ready for Jesus to take care of us. Her work was finished. I knew she had accepted our words, because God's radiant presence enveloped her as her spirit departed from her broken and lifeless body. Angels carried her to her eternal home.

In the days following her death, I felt wrapped in God's strength. However, the reality of life without Mom's reassuring presence soon set in. Those days were mixed with both sorrow and joy, but I still had my beloved Lizzie. I was carried by her love, by the love of God and by my dear friend Lynne, who had recently lost both her parents. Together we found our way through the maze of grief. Then without warning, just a few months later, I received the tragic news that Lizzie had suffered a massive stroke.

Once again, I made the sad journey from Boston to Lexington, to the same hospital where my mother had died. As I entered Lizzie's room, Alex, her husband, met me. He was crying uncontrollably. As we held each other, we prayed. A lifetime of memories flooded my mind. This gracious, loving woman had radiated kindness, mercy and love to everyone she met, but especially to my brother and me.

Lizzie had lovingly cared for J. C. and me like a mother with her own children. She was always there as we transitioned through the seasons of life. She was there through those unavoidable struggles during difficult times, as well as in the celebrations. She would wait for us on the back porch of her lovely home with tea and cookies, serving them up with a larger-than-life heart. Now that heart was struggling to survive. Her beloved husband had not left her side for a moment. I could sense that he desperately needed a break. Dad came into the room, and together we convinced Alex to leave for a while to take care of himself. Alex affectionately kissed "his girlfriend," as he always called Lizzie, and agreed to go with Dad for a brief meal.

As I sat beside the hospital bed, I held Lizzie's hand while I prayed quietly. I felt as though my heart would explode at any moment. My emotions were still raw from grieving the loss of Mom. I did not know how to respond to the fearful reality that I might lose Lizzie. I wanted to escape and get lost

Passing Peacefully through the Veil

A long-standing patient at my hospital had suffered for years from chronic leg pain due to poor circulation and neuropathy. He came in frequently for treatment, and whenever I asked how he felt, the answer was always the same. He felt terrible; the pain was unbearable. His condition continued to deteriorate for many years, despite numerous trials of medication and other pain management therapies. Every visit, his answer was the same, "I feel terrible."

Eventually, he landed in the ICU with a failing heart in addition to his leg pain. One morning as I made rounds on this very sick man, I asked for the umpteenth time, "How do you feel today?"

To my utter amazement, he said he felt wonderful and that all of his pain was gone. He went on to explain that three "nurses" dressed in white had been in to take care of him early that morning, and ever since then, he had been so much better. He then began, embarrassingly, to thank me for all I had done for him, and he followed that with a long, spontaneous praise of God.

After finishing my exam, I walked out to the ICU nursing station, which is centrally located so that no one can enter a room without being seen. I asked the nurses (who all wore green uniforms) if they had seen anyone dressed in white enter his room. They assured me that no one, other than themselves, had been there. This patient died peacefully and pain-free about two hours later.

—Anonymous

in denial—to shake off the fear and sorrow of this present moment. Darkness was descending on my soul. But then I remembered the countless times Lizzie had held me while I cried during numerous trials and heartaches—how her loving words and prayers had soothed my broken heart and how her delicate, cotton-embroidered hankies had dried my hot tears. I slowly realized that I had to remain by her side, as she had always remained by mine. I fearfully surrendered my heart to God in that moment and embraced the joyful sorrow of this time of holy transition with her.

Intuitively, I knew that Lizzie was leaving us. Opening my Bible, I began to read John 14 to Lizzie as she slept. Jesus said,

> In my Father's house are many rooms. . . . I am going there to prepare a place for you. And if I go and prepare a place for you, I will come back and take you to be with me that you also may be where I am.
>
> John 14:2–3

A profound grace entered my heart as I read aloud these comforting words. Jesus was coming to take His beloved Lizzie home. As my heart was emptied of the gripping fear, I felt an infusion of gratitude for the joy of having known this amazing woman. I spent the following few hours whispering my thanksgiving to her for all she had meant to me and to our family. It was a sacred time. The room, which was slightly darkened by the fading day, was suddenly illuminated by a brilliant white light. Without warning, Lizzie, who had been deeply sleeping ever since I had been with her, sat up in bed and lifted her arms toward the source of the light. Her face became radiant with a smile that erased the pain etched there just moments before.

I asked her, "Lizzie, what is it? What do you see?"

She answered with childlike joy in her voice, "Don't you see them?"

I asked again, "Who is it? Please tell me."

Without looking away from the vision, she answered, "On the mountain, I see my Jesus with His angels. He's calling me to come to Him. I've got to go. I've got to go! He's come for me."

Jesus was summoning Lizzie to Himself. It was a holy and breathtaking moment. My response was mixed with great emotion, but I agreed with her and said, "You're going home with your beloved—you've got to go to Him."

I believe Lizzie died in the arms of Jesus and was escorted by His holy angels to her eternal home. Alex was deeply saddened by her death, but he found great comfort in her vision and frequently asked me to repeat it to him. Later, even hearing it for the fiftieth time, he would gently nod his head and smile.

Elsie and Lizzie, these two strong, beloved women of faith, instilled in me a deep, joyful devotion to a good and generous God, a God rich in mercy and love, forever caring, providing graces needed in this life and beyond. For them and for me, the veil between this life and the next became thin. "Love never fails," 1 Corinthians 13:8 tells us. I learned this lesson firsthand from Mom and Lizzie—God's love goes on forever, without end. And in His endless love He provides the mighty angels, who help us and watch over us as His Kingdom becomes a reality here on earth.

Notes

Chapter 2: What Is an Angel?

1. John Calvin, *Institutes of the Christian Religion*, quoted in Billy Graham, *Angels: God's Secret Agents* (Nashville: W Publishing, 1994), v.

2. Martin Luther, *The Table-talk of Martin Luther*, trans. William Hazlitt, Esq. (Philadelphia: The Lutheran Publication Society, 1975), xvi.

3. Frank Newport, "Americans More Likely to Believe in God Than the Devil, Heaven More Than Hell," Gallup, June 13, 2007, http://www.gallup.com /poll/27877/americans-more-likely-believe-god-than-devil-heaven-more-than-hell .aspx.

4. Timothy Jones, "Rumors of Angels," *Christianity Today*, April 5, 1993, 22.

5. Billy Graham, *Angels* (Nashville: Thomas Nelson, 1995), 224.

Chapter 3: How Angels Appear

1. Billy Graham, *Angels* (Nashville: Thomas Nelson, 1995), 45.

Chapter 5: The Classification of Angels

1. Saint Teresa of Avila, *The Life of Saint Teresa of Avila by Herself*, trans. J. M. Cohen (London: Penguin, 1957), XXIX, 16–17.

2. Dionysius the Areopagite, *The Celestial Hierarchy*, quoted at http://www .tertullian.org/fathers/areopagite_13_heavenly_hierarchy.htm.

3. For more on this, see www.steliart.com/angelology_7archangels.html.

4. For the entire prayer, see http://www.ourcatholicprayers.com/the-saint -michael-prayer.html.

5. Pope John Paul II, *Regina Coeli Address*, April 24, 1994, quoted at www
.aquinasandmore.com/catholic-articles/who-is-st.-michael-the-archangel/article
/183.

Chapter 6: Guardian Angels

1. Georges Huber, "The Role of Guardian Angels in Our Lives," Catholic-
Culture, http://www.catholicculture.org/culture/library/view.cfm?recnum=3071.
2. Saint Jerome, quoted in "Feast of the Holy Guardian Angels," Living Water
Community, livingwatercommunity.com/saiints/holy%20guardian%20angels.htm.
3. St. Ambrose of Milan, *Letters*, 21-30, quoted at www.ccel.org.
4. From the *Book of Common Prayer*, quoted at justus.anglican.org/resources
/bcp/Muss-Arnolt/part4c.htm.

Chapter 7: Angels and Healing

1. Edward W. Desmond, "Interview with MOTHER Teresa: A Pencil In the
Hand Of God," *TIME Magazine U.S.*, December 4, 1989, http://www.time.com
/time/magazine/article/0,9171,959149,00.html.

Chapter 8: Unholy Fallen Angels

1. From the *Catechism of the Catholic Church*, quoted at www.catholicdoors
.com/catechis/cat0279, 391.
2. Billy Graham, *Angels* (Nashville: Thomas Nelson, 1995), 100.
3. Pope John Paul II, from a speech during his visit to the Sanctuary of Saint Michael
the Archangel, May 24, 1987, www.youtube.com/all_comments?v=gVtnRbhhgHk.
4. C. S. Lewis, *The Screwtape Letters* (New York: New American Library,
1988), xix.
5. Francis MacNutt, *Deliverance from Evil Spirits: A Practical Manual* (Grand
Rapids: Chosen, 1995), 183.
6. Billy Graham, "Angels All Around," *Decision*, December 1996, 3.
7. Francis MacNutt, *The Prayer That Heals: Praying for Healing in the Family*
(Notre Dame, Ind.: Ave Maria Press, 2009), 9. This book is an encouraging, practical
guide filled with wisdom for families, couples or anyone seeking a deeper prayer life.
8. Origen, *Against Celsus*, quoted in Evelyn Frost, *Christian Healing* (London:
A.R. Mowbray & Co., 1940), 160.
9. MacNutt, *Deliverance from Evil Spirits*, 46.

Judith MacNutt is president of Christian Healing Ministries, holds a master's degree in psychology from Eastern Kentucky University and is a licensed psychotherapist in Florida. As a clinical counselor, she discovered the need for prayer with her clients. After treating patients in state mental health institutions, Judith served as a missionary in Jerusalem for three years, directing a House of Prayer. There she worked with both Jews and Arabs. In 1977, Judith established Christian Counseling Services, integrating her work as a psychotherapist with healing prayer. She married Francis MacNutt in 1980, and together they founded Christian Healing Ministries. They have traveled extensively together and coauthored the book *Praying for Your Unborn Child*. Judith continues to travel and speak about the power of healing prayer. Judith and Francis live in Jacksonville, Florida, and have two adult children, Rachel and David.

If you have experienced the help and intervention of angels, Judith would love to hear from you. Please send your story to her at angelstories@christianhealingmin.org. Include your name, address, phone number and email address in case Judith would like to contact you about using your story as an illustration.